# GROUPWORK
# IN EDUCATION
# AND TRAINING

# GROUPWORK
# IN EDUCATION
# AND TRAINING

## IDEAS IN PRACTICE

MICHAEL REYNOLDS

KOGAN
PAGE

# To the memory of Gurth Higgin

First published in 1994

Kogan Page Limited
120 Pentonville Road
London N1 9JN

© Michael Reynolds, 1994

**British Library Cataloguing in Publication Data**

A CIP record for this book is available from the British Library

ISBN 0 7494 1027 2

Typeset by BookEns Ltd., Baldock, Herts.
Printed and bound in Great Britain by Biddles Ltd,
Guildford and King's Lynn.

# Contents

# Acknowledgements

I would like to thank the following colleagues and friends who have all helped substantially towards this book in one way or another – through influencing my ideas over the years, by commenting on drafts, by helping in its production, or by contributing to Chapter 7:

Tom Bier, Richard Boot, John Burgoyne, Ginny Hardy, Linda Harvey, Vivien Hodgson, Wendy Hollway, Pam Hosking, Annie Hudson, Gordon Lawrence, Bill Lytle, David McConnell, Jim McIntyre, Stephanie Parry, Stephen Potter and Jeffrey Rackham.

Thanks also to John Wiley & Sons Ltd for permission to reprint two figures from Boot, R L and Reynolds, M, 'Rethinking experience-based events', in Cox, C and Beck, J (eds), *Management Development: Advances in Practice and Theory* (copyright 1984, John Wiley & Sons Ltd.), and to Richard Boot for permission to include his Framework for Team Development.

I am indebted to the University of Chicago Press for use of the diagram in Figure 3.1, published in Robert F Bales's *Interaction Process Analysis*.

# Series Editor's Foreword

*Chris Bell, University of Plymouth*

Whether designing for face-to-face delivery, support materials, learning media or distance independent learning, there is need for much systematic thought, planning and evaluation. In practice, unfortunately, this is all too often not the case.

This series is designed to help those working in all areas of education and training apply the ideas of educational and training technology in order to produce the most effective and efficient instruction. The books are also appropriate for students studying education and training.

'Education and training technology', the overall theme of this series, is a much misunderstood (or not understood) phrase. In his book *The Concept of Educational Technology* (published in 1970 by Weidenfeld and Nicolson, London) Kenneth Richmond takes some 70 pages to discuss the meaning of the phrase. Numerous other authors have also spent many pages discussing the ideas from both conceptual and practical viewpoints. Definitions, often conflicting, abound.

It is my belief that the most valuable way of considering educational and training technology is to think in terms of the technology *of* education and training, and the use of technologies *in* education and training. The former, the less tangible, is very much a cross-disciplinary activity, drawing on anthropology, communications theory, learning theory, media research, psychology, sociology, statistics and many more areas. The latter is much more about the applications of hardware and software to the learning process.

In both cases, the focus is on increasing the quality (embracing both effectiveness and efficiency) of learning. Educational and training technology is concerned with the design, evaluation and assessment of the teaching and learning process (note the essential use of the term 'learning'). It is concerned with systematically analysing learning needs, relating these to relevant theories (and none too theoretically-based knowledge!) with the intention of optimizing learning. It is a rational, problem-solving approach to education and training.

Application of the ideas of educational and training technology is central to the improvement of education and training, to meeting the needs of learners, and to fitting the 'system' to these needs. At its best, it can provide a systemic, as well as a systematic, approach to the development and delivery of learning. The books in the series will help you do this, both from the perspective of the technology of education and training, and the use of technologies *in* education and training.

You may be wondering why a book about learning through groupwork has a place in the current series. *Educational and training technology* is about improving learning. The delivery of education and training is changing. Many educators and trainers are realizing that there are instructional techniques other than the lecture, laboratory, seminar and workbook. Wide-scale changes in the delivery of learning are starting to take place which some of the more enlightened have been advocating for many years. At last, we are seeing an increasing shift towards more learner-centred learning, towards an increase in flexibility, towards a recognition of the need for lifelong learning and increased learner autonomy. The appropriate use of groupwork can help deliver learning in this changing scenario; it can facilitate 'deep' as opposed to 'surface' learning, and can shift the emphasis from 'teacher as custodian of knowledge' to 'teacher as manager and facilitator of learning'. Michael Reynold's book will help you achieve this shift. It focuses upon the technology *of* education and training and, therefore, admirably meets my earlier criteria of being a valuable way of applying the ideas from educational and training technology in order to improve learning.

*Groupwork in Education and Training: Ideas in Practice* draws upon, and sets in a practical context, many of the ideas from the social sciences and from learning and educational theories which are invaluable to anyone involved in designing a quality learning experience, be it for traditional learners at university or college, learners in the workplace or social settings, or distance learners coming together for group study. It describes a range of ideas useful in designing group activities and in making sense of some of the consequences of using them. It is practical in nature, with a wealth of examples and case studies drawn from the author's experience of delivering learning through the use of groups.

# Introduction

An introduction to a book on groups or group behaviour could begin by claiming that interest in the topic is natural given the importance groups have in all aspects of work life and social life. Yet the preoccupation with group activities in training and education has not always been as pronounced as it may seem to us at the end of the 20th century. Interest has mainly been a feature of the last 50 years or so, and particularly since the 1960s. Knowing why is not only a question of curiosity, it helps us to make sense of the range of group activities currently available to teachers and trainers and the quite different reasons for using them.

My own introduction to groupwork from 1968 onwards reflects this growth of interest to some extent. I had been a student on a postgraduate course in organizational behaviour at the Massachusetts Institute of Technology. The entire course was based on a half-day session each week, in groups of 16, using experiential exercises backed up by selected readings. There were no tutors at these sessions. Two of the students in each group had attended the same session run by the tutors earlier in the week and now acted as group coordinators. This course proved very popular with the students and extra staff had to be drafted in to cope with the unexpectedly large numbers who signed up for a programme in organization development this course fed into.

On returning to the UK to teach organization behaviour to management students, I ran a very similar course, although for the most part I had more direct contact with the students than was the case in the original version. It seemed to go down well with the the students but not so well with some colleagues. After a term, the director of the programme called a meeting at which I was asked to explain why the students on my course spent most of their time meeting in groups, often with no tutor present and sometimes not even on the university's premises.

Within a year or two of this event students would joke that there was hardly a course in the timetable that was not based on groups of some kind. Finance and accounting, operational research, marketing, all had their version of groupwork. A change in preferred teaching methods was gathering pace, at least within management education.

My own influences at this time had, through the MIT programme, been mostly from the group dynamics school on which that course was based, supported by related work in sensitivity training and the move towards 'student-centred learning' incorporating the ideas of the American educationalist and psychotherapist Carl Rogers. On return to the UK I was fortunate to have a colleague whose influences were from the Tavistock Institute of Human Relations and, later still, through work with teachers in education, social work and community work, I had my approach to groupwork broadened by being challenged by more political, including feminist, perspectives. In the early 1970s I recall being invited to take part in one-day workshops to spread the word to school and college teachers around the country on how the Rogerian approach could (should!) be applied to *any* subject area.

# The scope of the book

This book is intended for thoughtful practitioners involved in education and training who use group methods or who intend to use them. It should also be of use to students of education or vocational training interested in the social, psychological or educational processes which can be encountered in working with groups.

There are many different *types of group activities* used in support of learning and in choosing examples throughout the book I have sought to illustrate some of the methods in common use without attempting to describe the entire range. Similarly, while there is an abundance of *theories* about groups, I have avoided greater depth in favour of showing the ways ideas differ from each other and the significance of these differences for anyone intending to use experiential methods.

Although there is also no shortage of ideas in the literature about the *social or political processes* encountered in education or training, such as socialization, or the way power or control effect or limit learning in the classroom and the wider context of educational institutions, applications of these broader social concepts to the practice of groupwork are harder to find. There has always been much more influence from psychological or psychotherapeutic theory with a focus on personal and interpersonal dynamics. (I hope to clarify this distinction between the psychological and the social or contextual significance of group behaviour in the first three chapters.)

With this in mind, in the second half of the book, and in the interest of restoring some balance between psychological and more sociological perspectives on groupwork, I have drawn mainly on ideas such as those which emphasize the way social values and beliefs are transmitted through educational processes – including the methods used, and on ways in which the social or organizational context can be reflected in the dynamics of the learning group.

Specifically then, the focus in these later chapters (4 to 6), is on such ideas as how the type of structure used in a group activity, or the amount of direction or control exercised, and the degree of choice offered to participants affects their experience and consequently their learning. I hope this will complement other equally relevant ideas on group behaviour such as roles, authority, leadership or patterns of interpersonal relationships which are more often written about.

*The overall purpose* of the book is to identify a range of ideas likely to be useful in designing group activities and in making sense of some of the consequences of using them. Above all, I hope to show how necessary it is to have ideas of some kind on which to base practice. In this way, while the book is not intended as a 'how-to', it is meant to provide the basis of practical guidance as well as giving a lead to some of the ideas and theories which have been developed in this field. There is a brief guide to further reading at the end of each chapter.

This book is certainly not written in support of dabbling. Group processes are complex and can have a profound influence over the learning and experience of those who engage with them. Teachers or trainers uninterested in understanding what happens in groups should probably stick to alternative methods. I hope that the chapters which follow will demonstrate the complexity of working with group methods but in a way that encourages their use.

## The structure

The first three chapters are about ideas and the next four chapters are based on practice. In Chapter 1, 'Why groups?', I describe some of the origins of groupwork because I find this helps to make sense of the various approaches to group-based learning encountered in education and training and of the different reasons for deciding to use them.

Chapter 2, 'Thinking about design' and Chapter 3, 'Making sense of groups', deal with ideas and models of group behaviour which are useful in designing group activities and in running them. With these three chapters as background, the next four are based on experiences of working with learning groups of various kinds.

In Chapter 4, 'Boundaries, predictability and control', I have used different examples of 'structured' group exercises to illustrate issues of choice and direction. Chapters 5, 'Learning from the milieu' and 6, 'Groups as open systems' explore the different ways group activities are inevitably influenced by, and reflect, the social context. In these two chapters the examples are of less structured activities.

I have chosen this format as a way of developing *ideas* about group methods by using different examples of them: the purpose being to make sense of a complex array of ideas, methods and issues without perpetuating oversimplistic assumptions that particular methods give rise to specific issues. So for example, questions of direction and control introduced in Chapter 4 and illustrated by structured activities are no less relevant to the more open methods described in the chapters which come after. In any case the notion of 'structure' is not as taken-for-granted as its common usage implies.

In Chapter 7, 'Groups in education and development' there are descriptions of four methods which illustrate the wider potential of groups in learning. These are the learning community, online groups, single-sex groups and team development. I have solicited comments on each of these from colleagues I know to be interested in them.

## Further reading

There are many books on group behaviour and many written about learning. It is more difficult to find any about learning from group methods. *Learning in Groups*, by David Jaques (1991) is especially useful in providing practical guidance to teachers.

# 1 Why Groups?

## Introduction

Groups of some kind have always been used for learning but there has been a considerable growth in interest in different forms of groupwork in education and training since the early 1960s. It is worth sketching out some of the earlier beginnings because it helps in understanding the different types of groupwork used at present and the underlying reasons for using them. Where did the group methods used in contemporary educational practice come from? Why has there been such a preoccupation with groups in both education and work?

The forms of groupwork used have developed from quite different origins, chiefly from group dynamics research, from psychotherapeutic and counselling group practice and, more broadly, from a belief in participative methods in education in support of democratic values.

In this chapter some of these origins are examined to provide a background to the theory and practice of groupwork which follows later. The first two sections are about the development of learning groups and the current preoccupation with group methods in education and at work. Following these sections are brief descriptions of various types of group methods, the ways in which they differ, and a summary of the different reasons for their use in education and training.

### The development of experiential learning groups

The most frequently recorded 'beginning' was in 1946 with the invention of the 'T (training) group' at a conference in Bethel,

Maine, USA. Thirty local community leaders (teachers, social workers and business people) met to work in three groups to discuss social problems of concern to them. The aim of the conference was to help these men and women develop the skills they needed to work more effectively in the community. A member of the training staff worked with each group and there was also a researcher present. The researchers, under the leadership of Kurt Lewin of MIT's Research Centre for Group Dynamics, were collecting observations on the interaction of group members to study the different ways the conference affected how delegates were able to transfer their learning 'back home'. In the evenings, Lewin would meet with his researchers and the training staff to analyse the data. Lewin apparently thought the participants should not be present at these sessions but some of them invited themselves.

The quality and interest of the discussions, as trainers, delegates and researchers jointly tried to make sense of the data and of the additional observations of the delegates, excited Lewin and his colleagues. As they wrote of it afterwards, they realized that by chance they had hit upon a powerful method of enabling people to develop their understanding of group behaviour and of themselves as group members. The 'T group', or 'Human Relations Laboratory' was the outcome, a method for learning about group behaviour and of developing group skills through the experience of being in one.

A few years before, though from a very different route, a similar development was taking place in England. Wilfred Bion, a psychiatrist, was conducting therapeutic groups for soldiers returning from the war. He used groups chiefly because most of the soldiers' difficulties were in relating to others. Bion believed that support and ideas from group members made this potentially a more useful approach than the more conventional one-to-one consultant-client relationship. This work provided the foundation for the later programme of study groups developed by members of the Tavistock Institute to help professionals in many kinds of organization learn about group and organizational processes, an approach which was to be widely used in higher education, though mostly within the social science and management areas. In 1967 the 'Intergroup' approach was added, enabling participants to learn about relations *between* groups and the effects of these relations on internal group dynamics.

Also from therapeutic origins in the mid-1940s, Carl Rogers was running groups for psychologists training as client-centred counsellors for American war veterans. Rogers became interested in the possibility of applying to education the same philosophy of 'group-centredness' that had seemed to work so well in the therapeutic setting, not only in the social sciences but in support of learning of any kind and at any level. He wrote up his ideas on student-centred learning in his book *Freedom to Learn* (1969), inspiring a good many educationalists to try out this approach, although not always as successfully as Rogers had hoped.

## The preoccupation with groups in education and at work

These starting points illustrate the sort of thinking and ideals which, in one way or another, have led to the use of groups in education. The role of therapeutic methods in all this may seem odd at first, but it illustrates the connections between learning, change and development, especially in the common interest shown by social scientists, educators and therapists in wanting learning to be grounded in personal and social experience and to be within the responsibility and, to varying degrees, the control of the individual.

Developing group methods for learning also answered the wish of many teachers for education to mirror and reinforce the values of democratic society. For all these reasons, groups came into their own as an educational approach. A group of people could make prior experience available for learning, could generate fresh material through experiential activities and could provide a forum for collective decision making about the content and direction of learning and development.

But that still does not explain why the development happened when it did, nor explain why most interest initially was shown in vocational and professional programmes. After all, games had been used to encourage learning long before they were established as an educational method in the 1960s; role playing was developed as early as the 1920s from Joseph Moreno's work with psychodrama; and, as Carl Rogers (1969) points out, interested educators have probably always looked for ways of getting their students more involved in their learning. The late Gurth Higgin, co-inventor of the intergroup exercise developed at the Tavistock Institute, believed that it was all part of the socio-economic change which followed World War II. Increased living standards gave people in the middle class in North America and Western Europe a greater interest in reflecting on the human quality of work, social life and relationships in general.

All this was matched by the growing emphasis on work group behaviour, begun in the 1940s and which stemmed from the famous Hawthorne studies in America (Roethlisberger and Dickson, 1939) and, later, from the Tavistock Institute's Longwall mining studies in England (Trist and Bamforth, 1951). These and similar studies provided the basis for a lasting preoccupation in organizations for developing group and team effectiveness through the application of group methods for education and training. Since those early days some of the pure forms of groupwork have had periods of decline, as Rogers, for one, suspected they might. Nevertheless, the principles which these approaches were based on still flourish in a range of experiential methods.

In the sections which follow, I will briefly describe some of the more familiar examples of group methods, introduce a way of distinguishing between them in practice and summarize the reasons groups are used in education and training.

## Types of group methods

• **Games and simulations**. I have included these together because they overlap so much in practice. In both, the aim is to recreate or represent in a limited time in the classroom particular situations which exist in the world outside. They may have a competitive element and may be based on someone's model of the way factors interact in everyday settings. Economics or business games are a good example of this kind, often using a computer program which incorporates the model on which the simulation is based. Alternatively, simulations can be free of any underlying model or framework. In Chapter 5, I describe a simulation where the intention is to provide participants with an opportunity to create a temporary organization on whichever model they choose. In either type, the purpose is to learn from the consequences of decisions and choices made within the exercise and to gain understandings which can be useful in the workplace.

An exercise often used in the selection of applicants for secretarial or administrative posts is to have them deal with a pile of memos while answering a number of telephone calls. This is an example of a simulation which can also be used in training. Simulations for training include research skills, interviewing, industrial relations and decision making.

• **Role plays** involve participants in taking roles and acting them out. The aim is sometimes to gain insight into unfamiliar roles in different situations (for example family, occupations, social groups), by trying to imagine and express the attitudes and feelings the people in them might have. Role play is also used to help people develop the skills and understanding they need in their work (interviews, negotiations, meetings, etc.) or, through role reversal, understand more of the other person's position in these situations. Participants may be given a detailed brief from which they act out the role, or may be asked to respond to the situation out of their imagination or experience.

• **Discussion groups**. These are the most familiar of all group activities (Hill, 1977). Yet some 'discussion groups' are little more than lectures with the lecturer sitting rather than standing. A discussion group, whether led or leaderless, ought to involve dialogue between group members or they are more an audience than a group.

• **Action learning** is used in organizations, mostly by managers. They learn by meeting in small groups or 'sets' at regular intervals to discuss individual work problems or projects. They are helped by group members and a consultant or 'set adviser'. The idea behind this method is that, in contrast to curriculum-based approaches, ideas are drawn in because they seem relevant to the problem or project (Pedler, 1983).

• **'Experiential exercises'** is often used as a generic term for many of the other examples in the list, especially games, simulations and role plays. More precisely, the term describes activities in which learning is by reflecting on observations and experience of a task specially designed for the purpose. The task can be simple in design – as in an exercise to show the effects of different group structures on the quality of interpersonal communication – or more elaborate, as in teams of participants having to build a raft to cross a lake in the course of an outdoor development programme. What they all have in common is that they generate material from which to learn in the 'here and now'.

Experiential exercises, also called 'structured exercises' or 'structured experiences', can be used to *demonstrate* particular ideas or theories, or to *generate* ideas from the students or trainees taking part. They are usually thought of as being quite prescriptive in focus, time, task and outcome. I will return to this assumption in Chapter 4.

● **T groups and study groups**. I put these together because they are both ways of learning about groups by being in one. T groups (sensitivity training) which commonly last for a week, are ways of learning about group dynamics and about oneself as a group member. Study groups have a similar focus and form part of 'Tavistock Conferences', together with intergroup and large group sessions. These 'conferences', which could last for a week or two, are based on the psychodynamic theories of people like Melanie Klein and Wilfred Bion. T groups on the other hand tend to have a more varied theoretical base, depending on who is working with them. As with some of the other methods, distinctions are easier to make on paper than sometimes make sense in practice.

As the ideas used in both these approaches are helpful in making sense of what happens in any form of learning group, they will appear in later chapters and in the Bibliography at the end of the book.

## Distinguishing between methods in use

It is tempting to draw up a more elaborate classification of the different types of groupwork in some system based on similarity or difference. Tempting, in the interest of order, but misleading. As I hope to make clear in later chapters, what makes this such a rich area for educators, students and scholars, is the variety of ways even the same basic method can be used in practice. So for example, in the preceding list you might say that study groups and T groups are examples of 'unstructured' groups and this would have some validity. The problem is that other methods such as role play or discussion groups may be equally unstructured depending on who is using them, and some T group facilitators may use quite structured role plays during the course of an otherwise less structured event. In any case, terms like 'structure' and 'direction' tend to be used as if their operational definition meant the same to everyone, which often is not the case.

## ILLUSTRATION:
### Interpreting 'structure' in group activities

A lecturer has put on a two-day workshop on research methods for a group of student teachers. It is intended as an introduction to the research projects the students are to carry out as part of the course. The lecturer favours what she has described as an 'unstructured' approach to the workshop. There is no pre-set agenda, no curriculum of research issues and there is no detailed timetable. Her idea is that during the two days the students will generate their own practical, methodological and conceptual questions and these will form the basis of subsequent discussion. She states her role as being to facilitate this discussion.

*What happens.* In this session the students are presenting their preferences for their project focus and methodology.

| | |
|---|---|
| *Student:* | I'd quite like to get involved in an evaluation of some kind. We've done a lot on teaching methods this term and I thought it would be interesting to compare say, lectures and case studies. |
| *Lecturer:* | What criteria would you use to make the comparison? |
| *Student:* | I'm not sure. I think I'd like that to come out of what students said about how they found the two methods, what they liked or didn't like, what they found useful or interesting, that sort of thing. |
| *Lecturer:* | But liking or not liking doesn't necessarily correlate with how effective the teaching method is. If you're |

interested in how much they've learned, surely you have to take account of the lecturers' objectives for the sessions and find out how much the students have picked up and understood.

*Student:* I was rather hoping to use very open-ended interviews. It's always interesting the comments that people make on their way out of a lecture. I'd like to capture some of that. Sort of build a picture up from our point of view … the students.

*Lecturer:* Yes, but interviews take a good deal of time to collect and analyse if you're going to be able to generalize from the data you collect. Will you be able to plan for sufficient numbers to make any comparison valid?

*Student:* Hmmm. It looks as though I need to think this through a bit more.

## Discussion

This was described by the lecturer as an unstructured workshop. In what sense is it unstructured? The design had no pre-set agenda or timetable and supposedly was not to be bound by a curriculum. But are these the only facets of structure?

The lecturer seems to hold very firm ideas on what she regards as appropriate methodology and, by the end of the exchange with her, the student is having doubts about a method which in most contexts would be regarded as an equally valid alternative.

Furthermore, in this brief extract at least, no other students take part in the discussion. It has become an individual tutorial with the others in the role of audience – a distinct and familiar structure whether it was planned that way or not. Through it, the lecturer attempts to influence how the student thinks about research and the way the project will be carried out.

To describe this session as 'unstructured' is misleading. It does not take all aspects of the emergent design into account and can give a false impression of how, for example, choice and influence are shared between lecturer and students. In some practical ways the workshop was unstructured but in this extract the *content* of the discussion was clearly being controlled by the lecturer. This relationship between structure and control is explored further in Chapter 4.

Rather than attempt some spurious classification of group methods, what is more useful for designing and using methods of any kind, is to be clear about the *ways in which they can vary* and the options which are available in design. Then, all group activities can, for example, be understood in terms of their *aims*, the *material used* for learning, or the *kind of involvement intended* for those who take part.

The *aim* might be to demonstrate a theory or idea. Some of the earliest experiential exercises in the social sciences were designed to repeat the research experiments which had led to the idea in the first place. For example, there are activities which can be used to demonstrate goal-setting and risk-taking behaviour of people with high 'achievement needs'. On the other hand, an activity might be used to explore or develop ideas in the spirit of 'lets see what happens if ...'.

Other types of aim might be to develop social skills or problem-solving abilities or, more broadly, to help participants understand the ways they relate to others in work or learning groups. Groups can also take part in the evaluation of a course, either when it's over or, more usefully, at an earlier stage while there is still time to make changes. They can even be involved in assessment of work when collaborative methods of assessment are used.

The *material* intended as the basis for learning can be distinguished as experiential, either drawing on people's past work or educational experience or, as in most games, simulations or structured exercises, generating fresh material for observation and analysis in the 'here and now'. Ideas — whether the tutor's, the student's or other people's — could be seen as a different source of material. In practice, ideas and experience are probably inseparable, but at least in the design the emphasis could be differentiated.

A further way of making sense of the ways group methods can differ is in terms of the *kind of involvement intended* for the students or trainees. Is the activity meant to be participative? How much choice over the nature and focus of the event is offered to those taking part? Are they meant to engage only their mental faculties, or are skills, values and emotional content also encouraged? How 'realistic' is the activity meant to be? On whose terms? What working relationships are staff and participants meant to engage in?

Distinctions such as these are only an indication of the differences between methods. The plan might be to work primarily with here-and-now material but there is nothing to prevent people making equally useful connections with past experiences as well. Even more problematic is whether the kind of involvement realized during a group activity is the same as was planned. However, even if these differences as to aim, material or type of involvement are not watertight enough to provide a basis for classifying group methods, they do serve as a useful reminder of aspects to be thought about in design, an approach which is developed in the next chapter.

# Reasons for using groups

The reasons for using groups can generally be summarized as motivational, educational, or ideological. There may be the belief that students will learn more easily because they are more involved, or that they can and should learn from each other and from the experience which can be generated in groupwork, or that learning in groups is preferable on social or political grounds – it is how people *should* work together. More often than not the reasoning will be some combination of these as Joyce and Weil (1972) write in *Models of Teaching*:

> The social models combine a belief about learning and a belief about society. The belief about learning is that cooperative behaviour is stimulating not only socially but also intellectually and, hence, that tasks requiring social interaction will stimulate learning. The belief about society is that a central role of education is to prepare citizens to perpetuate a democratic social order. (p. 215)

In other words, if learning is essentially a social process then using groups for learning is more likely to be effective than if it is limited to more individualistic approaches. Rationales such as these reflect the thinking which brought group methods into greater use and are worth going into in more detail.

**Motivational**. This, simply stated, is the view that people learn more when they are involved and enjoying themselves. Using games, simulations or similar activities is more memorable because they are more engaging. Taking part in them involves not only the mind; values and feelings are also brought into play. Learning under these conditions is more likely to 'stick'. Intuitively this makes sense but it has the same built-in limitation that 'involving' people at work does. Using groupwork as a motivational device may not work for long if students or trainees are looking for a more significant element of participation.

**Educational**. David Kolb, Irvin Rubin and James McIntyre, who designed the experiential programme in organizational behaviour at MIT that I described earlier, had a simple way of depicting this rationale. Their idea, in keeping with the student-centred philosophy they espoused, was that together, tutors and students examined and explored material in the spirit of collaborative enquiry. They used the diagram shown in Figure 1.2 to contrast this approach with the more traditional one of tutors passing onto students material which they, the tutors, had first developed or assimilated (Figure 1.1).

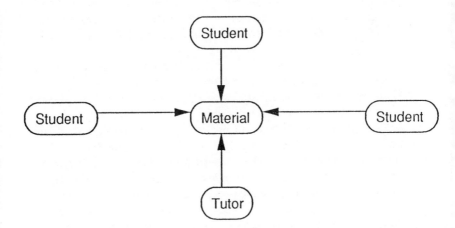

**Figure 1.1** *Group-based learning*

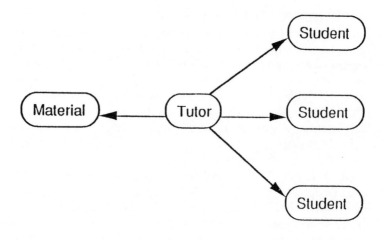

**Figure 1.2 Conventional teaching**

At the core of this approach is the belief that people can learn from each other as well as from teachers and that knowledge is constructed and reconstructed as a social process. It is not all 'out there' to be uncovered as 'truth'. Understanding in any field of enquiry is something which is constantly being created and negotiated and formal education should support that process through its methodology.

There are of course more obvious reasons for using groups when the aim is to learn about group processes, to develop the skills necessary in working with others in problem solving or planning, to gain an understanding of the difficulties which can arise in groups, or to develop self-confidence through expressing and defending one's own ideas. At the most practical level it takes account of the fact that at work people are members of task groups, project teams or meetings a good deal of the time. Learning in a group provides preparation for this.

**Ideological**. A further reason for using group methods in education is that this process of collective enquiry prepares people for a society based on democratic principles. Not only do people learn better this way, not only do these methods reflect more realistically the way knowledge is generated, but learning in groups helps develop individuals to be able to live and work participatively and to sustain a society based on those ideals.

John Dewey, who in 1910 wrote *How do we Think?* and in 1916, *Democracy in Education*, has had an enormous influence on liberal educators, particularly, but not exclusively, in North America. Authors advocating democratic or experiential approaches to learning and who for this reason emphasize groupwork of various kinds, acknowledge Dewey's influence. These include the 'de-schoolers', less positively described in more recent writings on education as 'new romantics'. However contentious this ideology might be in current school and college education, it has an immediacy in the context of training people for work. Are the methods used in their professional education likely to develop the sense of responsibility, imagination and cooperation which is expected of them in the workplace? I will return to this question in Chapter 5.

If these are the main reasons implicit or explicit in the interest in group methods, I suppose there might also be said to be a fourth category which could be described as **frivolous**, as in using group methods to keep students busy during a slot in the timetable where the teacher has forgotten to prepare anything else, or to give the them a 'good time', or to provide an excuse for using approaches tutors enjoy or are good at. And there is a fifth category − **getting it wrong**. It is unfortunate that some enthusiasts for groupwork give reasons which exaggerate the limitations of alternative approaches or make assumptions about them which are simply not true. Perhaps the commonest example is the description of lectures as a 'passive' form of learning. Sitting and listening during a lecture or case-study may not be physically active but the way people respond mentally to what they hear − making connections with other ideas and experiences − *is* active.

In this chapter I have described how and why group methods have come to to be so widely used in training and education and a way of making sense of what the differences are in methods or in the reasons for using them. In the next two chapters I will introduce some ideas which are useful in designing and running group activities.

## Further reading

For a more comprehensive study of educational rationale, *Models of Teaching* by Bruce Joyce and Marsha Weil (particularly the 1972 edition) looks at the ideas on which different teaching methods are based. There are chapters on role playing, simulations and non-directive teaching as well as other approaches not necessarily group-based, so comparison of method and philosophy is possible.

For an account of the way groupwork methods have developed see the introduction to *Small Groups and Personal Change* by Peter B Smith (1980).

There are many books and papers on games and simulations, some descriptive and some dealing with theory and issues. As a starting point, the journal *Simulation/Games for Learning* is a mine of information and references. It is the journal of SAGSET (now the Society for Interactive Learning). It contains articles which develop or review relevant theory and describe and/or evaluate exercises used in a wide range of settings, together with sources of materials, book reviews and reviews of similar journals worldwide. A 'must' for the student or practitioner working with group methods.

# 2 Thinking about Design

Learning groups involve more than an exchange of information and ideas. In a particular design, the relationships defined between students and between staff and students will affect how much is learned and the quality of learning. But more than that, these evolving social processes inevitably form part of the students' experience of the activity and, as such, provide an additional if often unintended source of learning, a concept I explore further in Chapter 5.

Designing a group activity or selecting from existing designs is therefore more than a matter of simply finding something appropriate for the intended topic or focus. It is also necessary to be aware of the values and beliefs expressed through the particular design and to understand the influences which it might have on the participants through the medium of the design itself. This is especially important if a reason for choosing a group-based approach in the first place is to help students or people on training courses develop the knowledge, skills and confidence to be able to enjoy membership of groups more generally.

This chapter describes a way of making sense of the complex relationship between design and participants' experience. In Chapter 3, the emphasis is on ideas which can be useful in understanding the processes of learning groups in practice.

## Models for educational design

There are models, both simple and complex, which attempt to formalize the process of designing for learning and which might be expected to apply to the specific case of designing group-based activities. Typically they follow the format shown in Figure 2.1:

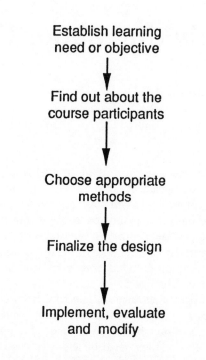

**Figure 2.1** *Model for educational design process*

But in practice, whether for groupwork or learning designs generally, does it really work like that? Apart from the implicit but questionable notion that once objectives have been sorted out, by choosing an appropriate method and using it competently you can *predict* what people will learn, this kind of model does not fully represent the more creative ways teachers or trainers come up with designs for learning.

A further problem in design is the way useful models of learning are mechanistically translated into the design of an activity or even a course. This is at least an attempt for the design to be informed by theory but may be a simplification of the learning process.

To illustrate, the 'Learning Cycle' described by David Kolb (1984) and others develops earlier ideas of the educationalist John Dewey into a useful model to explain how people learn through experience. Dewey believed that 'intelligent learning' came about through thoughtful reflection on the observed consequences and experience of events that 'happened' to someone or came about because of their own action.

Kolb elaborated these ideas into a cyclical model, not only to help understand experiential learning but later to explain the different preferences or 'styles' people reveal in how they go about learning. He emphasized the way learning prepared the individual to act differently on the basis of experience. Because of its emphasis on Dewey's ideas of learning from active experimentation, Kolb's 'cycle' has struck a chord with educators wanting to relate learning to experience and, as a result, has been very influential with those practising groupwork and other experiential methods.

Simply put, Kolb's cycle describes the way a person observes and reflects on their experience, planned or unlooked for, and makes sense of it in a way that leads to modified action in a similar situation in the future. The model is shown in Figure 2.2.

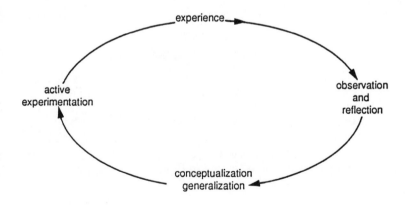

**Figure 2.2** *Kolb's learning cycle*

The model is sometimes converted into a framework for the design of an experiential activity for participants, as shown in Figure 2.3.

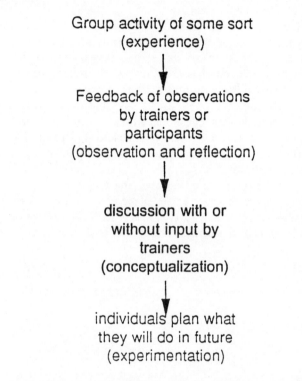

**Figure 2.3** *Conversion of Kolb's cycle into a design for an activity*

However, while Kolb's cycle is a useful way of conceptualizing the learning process, there are problems in applying it too rigidly as the basis of an educational design.

Trainers sometimes refer to 'going through the loop', or 'round the cycle' when using this approach. It is not that this design is not potentially useful; in fact it is similar to the design for 'outdoor' development used frequently in industrial training in which the approach is to help participants to reflect on the experience of carrying out group tasks of one kind or another.

The problem lies in applying it too literally in practice and the injustice this does to how learning actually happens. It can result in the different facets of the learning process being compartmentalized, as if observation, reflection or conceptualization are suspended until the appropriate part of the timetable and are absent during the performance of the activity. Equally misleading is the impression that while people are talking about observations or relevant ideas, experience is somehow absent. Usually these processes happen together; the 'discussion' is also a group activity and experienced as such by participants and tutors.

## Design as process

In practice, how often do educators follow something as orderly as these models suggest? For example, there must be times during a course when the best response to what has happened so far is to design a session from scratch.

Here is the kind of exchange which can take place between two trainers designing a session. It is based on an actual event in which a design emerged from an evening conversation between the two trainers in the 'back-of-an-envelope' tradition. It worked well and was used subsequently on other courses.

### ILLUSTRATION:

The course on methods in education was attended by 16 local education officers and further education teachers from the same region. The course had been based on short introductory presentations from the tutors, some practical demonstrations using group activities and group discussions. The conversation between the trainers was on these lines:

M: What are we going to do first session tomorrow?
R: Which one's that?
M: Evaluation. We didn't plan it in any detail because we said we'd wait to see how things were after the first four days.
R: What have we done before?
M: We've done whole modules on it for the MA but not just a

single session that I can remember.

R:  Why are we doing it?

M:  We agreed with Terry there'd be a slot on evaluation. It's something they're trying to encourage.

*Silence*

M:  There's all the educational stuff on formative, summative, illuminative. I find all that quite useful.

R:  I'm afraid I'm too tired to think after today. It seemed really uphill. And it must be nearly midnight.

M:  I'd rather know tonight than leave it until tomorrow.

*Silence*

R:  What about getting them to look at what they've done in the past they think has been good, and then use that to surface the criteria they're basing their judgements on?

M:  You mean like asking them 'but how do you know it worked?'

R:  Exactly. We start with getting them to think back to a session that they thought went well, they describe that in some detail, then we ask 'how do you know it worked?', drawing out their implicit yardsticks.

M:  What sort of groups? There's 16 of them.

R:  Two eights, or four fours?

M:  Four fours.

R:  Shall we mix them? The officers still don't talk to the teachers much.

M:  I think we should leave that to them. It'll be interesting to see if they come up with different criteria because of the different jobs they do.

R:  Then we'll bring everyone together to pool what's come out of it and finish up with a general discussion about methods of evaluation *we've* met or used and what we thought of them.

M:  Do you want to introduce it?

R:  I don't mind. If you introduce the final review session.

M:  Fine. And we could use the criteria that emerge from this session to review the week.

## Discussion

There are all kinds of design issues here – structure, direction, group composition, the tutor's role and there is some notice taken of the way the participant group has been working through the week. However, no other options are considered apart from a passing reference to previous work on the same topic. The design emerges from a shared approach, one which places the emphasis on drawing on people's experience and ideas through the minimal format offered by the tutors.

The detail had been intentionally left until a late stage in the course in order to take account of developments during the week. There is some risk in this approach of finding it difficult to be creative under the pressure of time but there is the opportunity for the design to be appropriate to the 'character' – in terms of discussion themes and ways of working together – the group has taken on. In this example, the basic idea was quite simple. It took minutes to design and minutes to introduce. How well it worked depended more on what happened in the session and the way of working staff and participants had developed with each other, than with the detail of the design itself.

Applying conventional models of educational design to group-based approaches is of limited value if they rest on the assumption that it should be possible to predict the outcome. This places too much emphasis on the design and not enough on what happens in its implementation. In the example above, a skeletal design was introduced towards the end of a course which had developed its own dynamics, relationships and life-history. Using groups in education involves so many complex processes that simple input-output models are inadequate. They fail to take account of the way people work and learn together, the relationships which develop and of participants as thoughtful, responsive, reactive, choice-making individuals likely to influence the outcome every bit as much as the initial design.

## Influences on learning outcome

There are many different factors which affect participants' experience and potentially their subsequent learning. This is clear from the reported experience of tutors and trainers who use group activities and of those who take part in them. There are the influences of the design itself and the social and educational philosophy expressed through its structure and methods, the roles defined for staff and participants, the kind of activity involved and the beliefs about learning and learning relationships implicit in all this. All these aspects of the design help to shape the exercise and the way participants will experience it.

Other factors also influence participants' experience and the outcome as well as those directly stemming from the design of the activity: expectations of groupwork based on prior experience or hearsay; individual interpretations of the tutor's intentions; participants' comfort in being members of groups in general and this one in particular; the way relationships have developed in the group to this time and the history of working together group members bring with them. Any of these and other factors can colour the experience of group-based designs and affect the learning outcome. Then there are cultural or occupational loyalties and differences, each person's state of mind during the exercise – including the tutor's – other courses attended by the participants and even the opinions expressed by other members of staff about this course, its tutor and its methods.

## ILLUSTRATION:

Two tutors on a training course for 18 voluntary organization administrators introduce an exercise in decision making.

*The aims are:*

- to compare decisions made by individuals with those made by a group;
- to develop decision-making skills.

*Method:*

- The tutors introduce the aims.
- Each participant is given a list of 'team characteristics' (see below) which they rank individually in order of importance. (Time allowed – 10 minutes)
- The group then meets to agree a ranking of the items. This should be on the basis of discussion so as to reach as much

agreement as possible rather than by averaging or voting. (Time allowed — 50 minutes)

• Discussion: the group members discuss how they reached consensus, how they feel about the quality of their decision-making process, what helped, what hindered, what part different members played, and so on.

---

## CHARACTERISTICS OF AN EFFECTIVE TEAM

On your own, rank these ten aspects of teamwork in terms of how important you think they are for an effective management team. Place the number one next to the item you think is most important, two by the item which is next important, and so on down to ten by whichever item you feel is the least important of all.

..... good communication skills

..... a sense of purpose

..... team members take initiative

..... a sense of team loyalty

..... conflicts are resolved without the team leader stepping in

..... knowledge of external demands on the team

..... clear objectives

..... an understanding of how groups work

..... an ability to deal with feelings as well as ideas

..... respect for the team leader

---

*What happens.* In the group ranking, there are a number of people who take no part. The mood of the others seems frivolous and, in spite of the ground rules, the task is rushed through and averaging is used for some of the items which attract little interest. The task is finished in less than 20 minutes, and is followed by a one-sided discussion with the tutors desperately trying to keep it going, raising observations and ideas about the group process which no one takes up.

*After the session* the tutors seek solace in the bar and try to work out what went wrong. Was the group too large? Should there have been two smaller groups, or one group but with some participants as observers? Should they themselves have facilitated rather than acted as silent observers? Should they have let the participants generate their own list of characteristics and should there have been more time for the individual ranking? Would it have worked better if there had been less time for the group ranking, creating more pressure to complete? Were the ground rules inappropriate? Should the exercise be scrapped?

**Discussion**
Decision-making exercises of this kind are in common use. The question in this example is whether the tutors are right in looking to the design for the explanation as to why the session proved such a disappointment to them.

Any of their questions about the design *might* have located the root of the problem. But equally, the outcome might have had nothing much to do with the design. Enquiring in a different direction might have revealed, for instance, that there was considerable resentment amongst the participants in being treated as 'managers' and seeing the tutors as attempting to indoctrinate them with unwelcome values from the world of commerce. Perhaps there was a history on the course of unresolved antipathy between members of two organizations who saw each other as rivals. Perhaps representatives of ethnic minorities on the course had felt patronized by the other participants and the tutors alike. Was the previous session implicated, in which the tutors had encouraged a degree of self-disclosure most course members thought inappropriate?

The point of this illustration is that the reason for an unsatisfactory session might have nothing to do with its design. Other factors such as people's expectations, prior experience of the course, attitudes towards each other or to the tutors might be the reason it went as it did. Directing their effort to examining and modifying the design could have been misplaced.

Figure 2.4 shows *some* of the many different factors which can be involved in using groups, including the design process itself. It helps identify overarching principles — such as who controls the various aspects of design and what values and beliefs are introduced about how people should be able to work together or how they learn, often implicitly present but seldom stated. It also illustrates the limitations of attempting to predetermine the learning outcome simply by modifying the details of design.

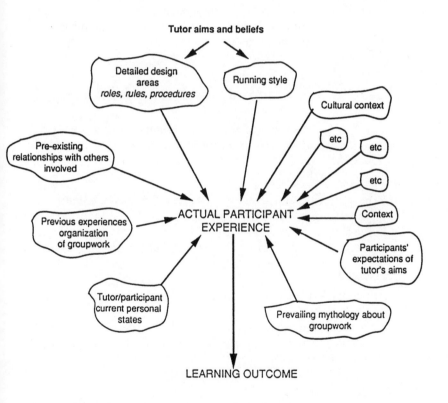

**Figure 2.4** *Factors affecting the experience and outcome of learning groups* (Modified from Boot and Reynolds (1984) and used with the publisher's permission)

In planning experiential approaches it is perhaps more useful to take account of the processes engaged in working with groups than to apply linear models which ignore them. The way to get the best from a design is through the way of working with participants, of helping them work together as a learning group and to make sense of what happens during it.

In the evaluation design for the educationalists I described earlier in this chapter, the design itself is very simple but the outcome can prove richly complex. *It is in working with the design in practice that attention to detail becomes important.* After all, much can be learned from a design which 'went wrong' if tutor and students are prepared to do so.

# Questions in planning for learning groups

The sort of questions which are useful in thinking out a design for a group-based activity, or in trying to understand why it seemed not as useful as it had promised, are of this kind:

- **Purpose**
  What is the purpose of the session? What learning opportunities are to be created?
  Is the aim of the session to illustrate pre-selected ideas, or is it an opportunity to explore and develop ideas from the activity?
  Is the 'process' more important than the 'product'?
- **Context**
  What session will they be coming from? Where do they go next?
  How does this session link with other parts of the course? What support/understanding is there from other tutors/ trainers/departments?
  What will follow for the participants?
- **Design**
  Is there a suitable exercise available or is there a need for something new? What information do the participants need?
  Should the session draw on prior experience or generate shared experience in the here-and-now?
  What is the time available? Is there enough time to deal with

any unforeseen outcomes?

How much structure does the session need? Is there enough flexibility to work with whatever connections/associations/questions the participants come up with?

Given the numbers, their history to date, the task and the time available, what group size seems best? Is there a role for a facilitator? If so, what should that be?

- **The group and its history**

  Is this a new group? What differences are there of culture, gender, class or occupation? Is what is to be asked of them likely to be acceptable?

  If this is not a new group, what have things been like so far? What has happened in previous sessions? What subgroups are there, and what relationships seem to have developed, with what tensions, conflicts or alliances?

  How do I/we, as trainers/tutors seem to be getting on with them? Do we know?

- **Overall**

  How will the session be evaluated?

  What will be the criteria for its success?

  Should we be thinking this out on our own, or would it be better to be talking it out with participants?

In this chapter I have introduced ideas about the process of design, concluding with some of the questions I find useful in planning or in later review. Others may have different sets of questions which work well for them.

The next chapter describes ways of making sense of what happens in group activities. It is longer than this one, which reflects my belief as to where the attention to detail should lie.

## Further reading

One of the most thorough discussions of learning theory which can be applied to groupwork is *Experiential Learning* by David A Kolb, (1984) referred to in this chapter. Kolb develops his ideas drawing on research and other authors. The book is valuable as a source of references. A shorter account of the 'Learning Cycle' can be found in *Theories of Group Processes*, edited by Cary Cooper

(1975). In this useful collection of papers there is one by Kolb and R E Fry, 'Toward an applied theory of experiential learning'.

For ideas about design as such, Don Binsted's papers present a systematic approach to design for management developers which elaborate the 'need-design-implement' model. Influenced by Kolb and by organizational development work, they are a helpful reminder of the different factors to consider through the design process. 'The design of learning events for management, parts 1 and 2', *Management Education and Development*, 1980, 1981.

By way of contrast, the ideas I introduced in this chapter, emphasizing that factors other than design affect the outcome of experiential learning events for participants, are argued more fully in 'Rethinking experience based events' by Richard Boot and Michael Reynolds, in *Management Development: Advances in practice and theory*, edited by C Cox and J Beck (1984). The section 'Distinguishing methods in use' (Chapter 1) also draws on this work.

# 3   Making Sense of Groups

## Introduction

At an early stage in my career as a lecturer using group methods, a psychologist I worked with commented that he had no sense of the theoretical framework I was drawing on. This indicated a fundamental difference in the ways in which we each applied theories about groups to our educational practice. The difference was that whereas his interpretations were based on a single coherent set of ideas – a psychoanalytic framework with which his observations and actions were totally consistent – I looked to a number of frameworks, including the one he worked from.

Implicitly, the principle which influenced my approach to groupwork was that there were various ideas from disparate schools of thought which could be of value in making sense of group activities. A second distinction being made between us was whether theories were more useful for being made available to students to help them develop their own understanding, than being presented as unarguable 'truth'.

Something we did agree on was that it was important for teachers and trainers who work with group methods to be clear about the ideas and assumptions, values and beliefs which inform their practice. But I am doubtful of the view that there is any one school of thought which should have pre-eminence. Professionals engaged in groupwork differ on this and on the ideas about groups which they regard as valid. The purpose of this chapter and the book as a whole, is to emphasize the value of ideas from different sources used thoughtfully, rather than to encourage doctrinaire adherence to a particular theory.

Theories about groups vary a good deal, from the popular to the obscure. Some are simple to grasp but fail to do justice to the complexity of life in a learning group, some seem more powerful as explanations but can be very difficult to understand. Some seem to deny the dynamics of groups altogether.

Group theory has been developed in pursuit of different interests too. Some social psychologists studied group behaviour in the hope of understanding and redressing social injustices such as racial prejudice or extreme authoritarianism, as for example, Solomon Asch's (1952) experiments on group conformity. Other theories were developed from the increasing use of groups for psychotherapy or – as with Ronald Lippit and Ralph White's (1958) experiments on leadership styles, or Alex Bavelas's (1951) investigations into different communication patterns – from an interest in group behaviour in work.

The focus of some theories is the individual or the interactions of group members. The Interaction Process Analysis scheme developed by Robert Bales (1950) is an example of this focus and is described in a later section of this chapter. Others stress the context, the social or political processes which are carried into the life of a group, a reminder that even defining a 'group' as such is itself an interpretation. Ideas of this kind form the basis of Chapters 4 to 6.

There have been differences in methodology also. Much of the early work in social psychology was based on experiments with undergraduates, an approach which lost some support when it was appreciated that the research 'subjects' felt inclined to help the researchers by providing them with the results they thought were hoped for. In contrast, some of the most influential ideas from psychoanalysis have been the result of thoughtful reflection on the experience of years of clinical practice.

But the relevance of a group theory is often broader than the context in which it was formulated. A theory emerging from psychoanalytic practice can also help us understand the dynamics of work groups or learning groups. With this in mind, I will look at theory in terms of the ways it can be used in educational practice.

A way of summarizing how teachers or trainers can apply theory to working with learning groups, is to think in terms of three related activities:

'Picking it up' – observing or experiencing what people seem to be doing or saying.

'Making sense of it' – analysing or interpreting the observations.

'Doing something about it' – using the observations and analysis to intervene in some way – or deciding to do nothing at all.

In the rest of the chapter there is a selection of approaches to observing and interpreting group behaviour. They are divided into observation guides ('picking it up') and explanatory frameworks ('making sense of it'), followed by an illustration of how some of these ideas might be applied in practice to a group activity. The chapter ends with a summary of some general principles I have found useful in working in the area of experiential learning.

# Observation guides

There are many examples of lists – often that is all they are – to help in making observations of groups. Here is one I have found useful in introducing students to the basic idea that it is interesting and useful to have a guide to observation. It can be used to review progress in the group or it can provide the basis for deeper explanations of group process depending on what the purpose of the activity is:

- *Communication*
  Who talks to whom, who supports whom?
  Who seems actively involved? Who doesn't?
- *Decision making*
  How are decisions and choices made?
  Who is involved in this and in what way?
- *Power and influence*
  What seems to be the basis and pattern of power and influence in the group? Does it change over time?
- *Conflict*
  How are conflicts of ideas, opinions or interests worked out

within the group? Are they resolved and if so how?
● *Ethos*
What does it seem to be like to belong in this group? Are there accepted norms of behaviour? What roles or rules develop?

This observer guide is quite old, its origins probably in the materials handed out at a National Training Laboratory T group (see Further Reading, p. 63). It is a simple device with not much in the way of an underlying conceptual framework but it gives a guide as to what to look for and underlines the idea that what you see or experience in a group is not random but has meaning. The patterns which can be observed are significant and can be helpful in understanding and developing the way group members work together.

Observation guides like these can be converted into simple rating scales and used to evaluate group performance, ideally by using them as the starting point for a discussion by group members. Even better is to get the group to construct a list of items which reflect their own views about what they would like the characteristics of their group to be and then use it to evaluate how they worked together. The resulting instrument might be of this kind:

How effective was the group in problem-solving?

\* — — — \* — — — \* — — — \* — — — \*

Ineffective                                        Effective

Did people seem to trust each other?

\* — — — \* — — — \* — — — \* — — — \*

Not a lot                                        Completely

How were decisions made?

\* — — — \* — — — \* — — — \* — — — \*

By a minority                                        Shared

How was leadership exercised?

\* — — — \* — — — \* — — — \* — — — \*

By one person                    Spread around

Through discussion, vague notions like 'effective' or 'leadership' can be elaborated in the context of the group activity and the beliefs of group members, rather than being used as if there were universal definitions everyone was supposed to share.

## Bales' categories for observing groups

Perhaps the best known example of an observation guide for understanding group behaviour is the category system developed in 1950 by Robert Bales. Bales, a Harvard sociologist, wanted to find out why Alcoholics Anonymous was so successful in helping people with drink problems. He invited himself to AA meetings but the organizers wouldn't let him ask questions for fear of disrupting the discussions. Bales compensated for this by scribbling notes on what he heard and began to see patterns in the way people talked and in the way they responded to what others had to say. These patterns formed the basis of his categories of interaction (see Figure 3.1).

Bales' scheme makes the distinction between behaviour directly related to the task (giving suggestions or opinions), and behaviour more concerned with the social processes which help or hinder the group working together (social-emotional area, eg joking, agreeing, showing antagonism). As with the earlier guide, this is an important example of a scheme designed to study group *process* rather than the *content* of the group's discussions. There are other aspects of groups which Bales' scheme does not cover: what people were *actually* thinking or feeling; the content of the task itself; the purposes, intentions, previous relationships and so on. But it is a useful introduction to what can be observed and analysed in a learning group.

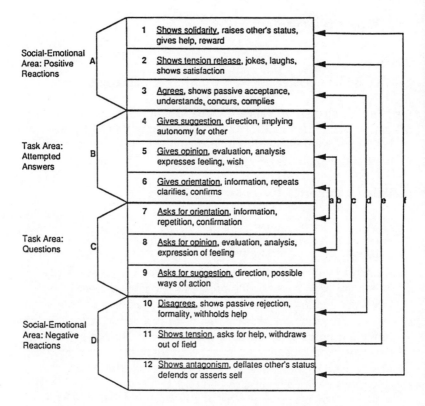

The system of categories used in observation and their relation to major frames of reference

Key:
a Problems of orientation
b Problems of evaluation
c Problems of control
d Problems of decision
e Problems of tension-management
f Problems of integration

**Figure 3.1** *The system of categories used in observation and their relation to major frames of reference* (used with the permission of the University of Chicago Press, © Robert F. Bales, 1950.)

## Some points about observer guides

Bales' system illustrates some general points to be aware of in applying schemes of this kind:

- His claim is that the scheme is universally applicable, yet it was developed using problem-solving groups in experimental settings using a laboratory and one-way mirrors. Furthermore, if the language of his early papers is anything to go by, all the participants were men.
- The scheme has a strongly normative flavour to it. 'Goodness' or 'effectiveness' are narrowly interpreted in terms of performance or production, outcomes which might be expected of problem-solving groups. These definitions are not necessarily as applicable to group activities of a different kind, especially those designed for learning.
- Finally, there is a significant difference between Bales' framework and the observer guide I described earlier. They are both based on the idea of group 'processes' but the observer guide, though simple, keeps open the possibility of interpretations of *social* as well as *interpersonal* dynamics. The drawback of Bales' system is that it can be used to impose on the situation a scheme for understanding groups in terms of interpersonal interaction alone. In so doing social, political or cultural processes could be obscured.

# Explanatory frameworks

This section describes three different examples of theories of conceptual frameworks which can be used to interpret what happens in learning groups.

The first emphasizes the idea of *stages of development* and has become well established with trainers who use group methods. The second, less accessible perhaps but worth the effort required to understand it, is a way of making sense of what happens in groups by taking account of *unconscious forces* which influence outward behaviour. The third is a way of thinking about group behaviour in terms of inevitable *dilemmas* people face when working together. It draws on a broad range of ideas, psycho-social and political, while also allowing for unconscious processes.

Each of them can be applied to groups of any kind, including groups for learning. They go further than observer guides in that in different ways they attempt to *explain* why groups behave the way they do.

## Stages of group development

One way of making sense of the sometimes bewildering events which occur in group life, is to assume that there are stages through which a group must develop in reaching a state of 'maturity'. The best known version of this is the scheme put forward by Barry Tuckman (1965). It illustrates well both the idea of group development and the problems in accepting it without reservation.

Tuckman's is a linear model, some say hierarchical. A group passes through the first stage on to the second and so on until reaching the final stage as an effectively performing group. There are other models which are cyclical, early stages of development being returned to as the life of the group evolves. Tuckman's approach was to bring together numerous studies by other researchers. He came up with four stages of group development which he described as follows:

FORMING:    exploring what the group will be like, finding the basis of forming relationships with others. Finding out who they are, acceptance of whoever is in the formal leadership role.

STORMING:   conflicts break out as subgroups emerge, differences are confronted, control becomes an open issue and is resisted, regardless of its source ... including a formal leader.

NORMING:    rules start to emerge about acceptable ways of behaving and of carrying out the task of the group; these rules are applied in working with conflicts and a spirit of cooperation develops.

PERFORMING: conflicts are resolved, energy is put into task accomplishment – the group is becoming effective.

Tuckman was actually quite critical of the idea of producing a generalized theory to apply to different types of groups in different situations. The research studies he reviewed were varied in methodology and he was unhappy with the approaches taken in some of them. However, in spite of his warning, this model is widely known and applied by people using groups nearly 30 years later. Its limitations are, as other researchers have pointed out, that it is a simplification. Not all groups follow these stages exactly and no allowance is made for the context and history of a particular group, who the people are and what their task or purpose is.

## Some points about development models

Helpful to a point, generalizations like Tuckman's model of group behaviour can be misleading if applied too rigidly. The idea of groups developing in *some* way seems realistic and his descriptions are familiar to most people's experiences of groups. But applied simplistically, models of this kind can obscure what is really going on and even draw attention away from the tutor's responsibility. A group of dissatisfied participants can indicate that something is wrong with the course or the way it is being run. Trainers talking about 'counter-dependency' or describing a group as 'well into the storming stage' could be missing the point. What *they* are doing or not doing could be the problem. Group theories should be used to illuminate the dynamics of the group, not to cover up tutors' limitations.

A further point Tuckman's model illustrates is that theories are seldom, if ever, value-free. Themes of effective performance and conflict resolution are more applicable to some types of group activity than others and indicate particular, not universal, ways of seeing the world. As Marion McCollom, one of the authors I recommend for further reading, points out, Tuckman's concern with performance may have had as much to do with the fact that his research was funded by the US Navy as with the research material he examined. It would also explain why the model is so popular in management training.

But it is easy to be critical. If we waited for ideas to be critic-proof before they were disseminated, the bookshelves would be empty. What is important is to be aware of how useful even the simplest model can be but how easily it acquires the status of unquestionable and universal truth – especially if it takes the form of a list, or better still, a cycle, matrix or pyramid. Models of this kind are easily assimilated and will last for decades regardless of contradictory research or the warnings of the authors themselves. Tuckman's model is useful in emphasizing the possibility that development of some kind takes place in groups and it can serve as a way to begin to explain what we see or experience in them.

## Taking account of unconscious group processes

In this section I will introduce some of the ideas developed within psychotherapy and psychoanalysis, particularly those of Wilfred Bion. Bion's ideas have had a profound influence on research and practice in using groups and are relevant for understanding groups within education and training.

There are some excellent summaries of Bion's ideas and I have included those by Barry Palmer and Margaret Rioch in the suggestions for further reading. In the educational world these ideas are not given the attention they deserve, perhaps because of their complexity, perhaps because of their association with psychoanalysis. But they are essential reading for anyone working with groups because they try to make sense of processes which will inevitably be encountered.

The central idea in Bion's way of understanding groups is that it is as if in the life of any group, regardless of its function, there are actually two distinct groups. The first group is the 'work group', putting its energies into the task its members have met to perform – constructing, debating, organizing, arguing, with moments of excitement, frustration, disappointment, triumph and all the other things we associate with collective work. But there is also a second 'shadow group' that from time to time takes over.

The shadow group may *appear* to be working on the task but is actually governed by powerful yet unconscious emotive forces arising out of fears for individual or group security. Bion called this group the 'basic assumption group' because its members act 'as if' certain things were true even though they are not. Barry Palmer describes it as a 'survival group', which I find useful because that describes *why* people are behaving as they are. In essence, the group members in this state are in the grip of primitive and pervasive doubts brought on by the uncertainties of their situation. Will the group survive? Will individuals become marginalized or lose their sense of belonging? Will their individuality be engulfed by the group? Will they feel taken over by it?

Bion described three basic assumptions which his experience as a therapist led him to believe could be present in a group. Their purpose at an unconscious level is to make group members feel less insecure. However, this is spurious, an emotional response to uncertainty, to what is imagined, and distracts group members from the reality of the work to be carried out, including any critical examination of its actual problems. What it does, is to replace intolerable levels of uncertainty with something which seems more manageable.

Using Barry Palmer's terminology, the assumption groups are called 'dependency', 'expectancy' and 'fight-flight':

*Dependency:* group members act as if they have no ideas of their own, are vulnerable and lack any basis for initiating action. They seem dependent on leadership from the person 'in authority' or, if that doesn't materialize in an acceptable form, from someone thrown up by the group itself.

*Expectancy:* similar to dependency, people seem to live 'in hope' that a leader, or some new approach or galvanizing idea will arise which will ensure the group's survival.

*Fight-flight:* a term of Bion's most of us have heard even if we haven't read *Experiences in Groups*. The group members act as if they can hold something or somebody responsible for everything that makes them feel insecure and they must either fight it off or run away from it. But the important thing is to be doing something, whatever it is.

*Some points on Bion's ideas*

I am unlikely to have done these complex ideas justice in such a brief summary but hopefully demonstrated how Bion's descriptions are useful in giving an idea of ways groups facing uncertainties of this kind might act. Their value is in illustrating the possibility of groups having this other, anxiety-driven way of behaving, as distinct from the work-group mode its members are striving for.

In groups which are less directed or less structured than has been traditional in education, these uncertainties will be present from time to time, and the less structured the activity the more likely it is that this will be so. Moments where participants are asking for information they already have or for levels of guidance that seem to deny their own capabilities; times when they seem to assume unrealistic powers on the part of the teacher or trainer; resorting to blaming others for their frustration – all these can be manifestations of a group that has slipped into survival mode.

In spite of the language and to some extent the tone of these ideas, they are not intended to belittle or demean. The intention is not to portray group members as weak, inadequate, or as 'child-like'. On the contrary, effective groups of thoughtful, responsible, committed participants can experience these 'survival' group modes if faced with enough ambiguity. Neither is it intended to depict some 'stage' of immaturity in the development of the group. It is a way of making sense of a response to uncertainty – initially subconscious – and it can happen at any time.

## Group dilemmas

In an unpublished paper, Stephen Potter describes 'A Framework for Understanding Groups Generally' (see also Potter, 1978). It is an overarching set of principles into which specific theories about group behaviour can be subsumed. The main idea is of the dilemmas which each person faces as a member of a group. He wrote about the framework in this way:

Broadly from the literature on group dynamics and groupwork methods of all kinds, the group can be usefully understood as a meeting of people ... bounded by the following three dilemmas:

| | |
|---|---|
| *First Dilemma* | Establishing and maintaining oneself in the group which raises dilemmas as to openness-closure: intimacy-distance: security-insecurity; role-person. |
| *Second Dilemma* | Establishing and maintaining the primary task, member-group relations to the task; justifications and ideologies supporting the task; criteria for knowing when it is done and from learning from doing it. |
| *Third Dilemma* | Establishing and maintaining some form of management, leadership or politics for the group. |

Varying degrees of awareness about these dilemmas and varying interpretive models as to the interaction of solutions to these dilemmas abound in social science, group dynamic and groupwork literature.

I have found the notion of dilemmas appealing because it considers people as thoughtful and purposeful, largely responsible and acting out of their wishes, beliefs and values. It is also very practical because it can be translated into the questions anyone can find themselves asking when belonging, or wanting to belong, to a group; questions which fit the experience of being in work groups, learning groups, families and social groups, such as:

What is it going to be like for me in this group?
What might I have to give up to be a member of it?
Where will my support come from?
Will my right to privacy be respected?
Will I always know what's going on?

What are we supposed to be doing, why, to what end, who says so?
What am I supposed to be doing?
What rights do I have in determining that?

Who can I trust?
Where do I look for guidance?
How much influence will I have over what happens?
Will I be able to do what I want to do?
Will I have others I can depend on?

In the context of a learning group, particularly when learning is more than acquiring ideas or facts but may involve challenging or disconfirming assumptions about our values, beliefs or the image we have of ourselves, there is a further dilemma: there is a tension between wanting to learn, develop, see things differently, and the need to hold on to the ideas which have seen us through, more or less, up until that point.

# Ideas in practice

So far, I have introduced just a few of the different ways people have tried to make sense of what happens in groups. In this final section I will use an example of a group exercise to show how different frameworks might be applied. There is then a summary of some general guidelines I believe can prove helpful in using group methods with course participants.

## ILLUSTRATION:

I had been asked by a colleague to work with her to introduce some experiential sessions into a social psychology course she was teaching for undergraduates in applied social studies. One of the activities was designed to focus on the processes encountered in organizing and carrying out work. We called it, simply, 'Designing tasks for others'.

The students, 20 in number, were asked to divide into two groups. Each group was to design a task which the other group would carry out. There was to be an hour and a half for this, leaving a further half-hour for discussion.

The two groups formed and left for different rooms with one of us as observer/facilitator in each. Ideas for the tasks to be carried out were discussed and it seemed as if plenty of material was being generated from which to examine ideas about decision making, communications, intergroup activity and the consequences of different ways of organizing work.

Halfway through the session there was a coffee-break. The students went off to the canteen and we stayed behind to compare notes on how the exercise had been going. After a while, the entire group returned and crowded into the room we were sitting in. We were told by one of the male students that as far as they were concerned the exercise was over. They were not going to design any tasks, so there would be no work for anyone else to carry out.

Things had seemed to us to be going quite well up until this point; different from other groups we had worked with using the same activity perhaps, but that was part of the value of this exercise − there was scope for participants to interpret it in different ways. What had gone wrong? Why were the students apparently rejecting an opportunity to learn something about organizational process in a lively and interesting way?

It became clear that as future social and community work students, the learning they were interested in was to explore and understand the consequences of resisting formal authority, represented in this instance by the tutors. For the rest of the session we were able to draw on our own and the students' observations and experience of the incident. We discussed the social and political significance of what had happened and its parallels in the wider social context.

Using this example, how might the different guides and frameworks have been useful?

**Discussion**
In the first part of the session, observer guides of what to look for in groups were useful. In activities like this, they can be given to participant-observers at least, if not to all the students taking part. The observations made could be used, either at the time or later in discussion, to piece together patterns which emerge in the way the groups are working and help explain what they mean.

Observations are not explanations even though what you see or hear is likely to reflect the interpretative ideas you favour. For example, looking for patterns in who talks, who replies and so forth, may indicate beliefs in a group about how work should be carried out and decisions made, or it may reveal something more fundamental, as in culturally defined expectations of different roles for men and women. So, in the same way, using Bales' interaction categories may show the way different people agree, contest, support, etc. but it could also be used to show that 80 per cent of what was being said was by the men in the group.

It is worth emphasizing that although the exercise in this illustration was intended to provide an opportunity to learn about social processes in the work context, the value of looking, listening and making sense of what can be seen and heard is just as relevant to a project group in geography or a tutorial in English literature; either in the secondary interest of developing participants' ability to work in groups, or because there is a problem with the way people are working together which is limiting their learning of geography or literature. It is also useful to learn to observe and understand group process as a member of the group. The role of participant observer can be difficult but is good practice for the real thing.

Observer guides could still have been useful after the coffee break. How representative was the spokesman? How significant was it that it was one of the men? Adopting ideas about stages of group development might suggest this was a phase of 'storming', rejecting or at least challenging the tutors' authority. Using the notion of unconscious forces in the group, had the exercise been unstructured enough to tip the students into some form of collective 'survival' state, manifested in a contest with the tutors?

In this illustration, Bion's ideas are useful. They would confirm that what was going on was 'real work'. The actions the students took were in the interests of learning, which was the primary task of the group. The tutors were being involved in this but in a different way than they had expected. While reasonable to *consider* the possibilities of counter-dependency, storming, or fight-flight, on this occasion making interpretations of this kind would have distracted from the opportunity the students were creating out of the exercise they had been presented with.

# Some guidelines for working with learning groups

In this chapter I have described ideas which I have found useful in running group activities or which are well known and help to provide an overall picture of the types of ideas and frameworks which are available. Some well known theories, like transactional analysis, are missing from this account which I suppose reflects my opinion of them as too interpersonally orientated to help much in illuminating *group* behaviour.

Also there are other, more general ideas, which are relevant in using learning groups. For example, Malcolm Knowles' and Carl Rogers' writings on adult learning, Paulo Freire's ideas on education which, though set in a very different context, describe ways of defining student and teacher roles which seem particularly appropriate to learning in groups rather than in more conventional lecturer-audience mode. I have included these authors in the bibliography.

To conclude this chapter I will summarize some *rules of thumb* which I find useful when working with group methods. They are not theories, more in the nature of principles which can guide the application of whichever theories and models seem relevant. They are organized within the simple framework introduced earlier as 'picking it up', 'making sense of it' and 'doing something about it'. Some of them will be developed in later chapters.

## Picking it up

The strongest reason for *taking note of group processes*, apart from interest in learning about them for their own sake, is because the purpose of the activity is being limited or even undermined in some way. It is perhaps more usual in the classroom and in other social settings to notice something is wrong yet not comment until afterwards — if at all. As a conference delegate remarked when it was clear to all but the organizers that people's interests were being frustrated by the programme: 'You ignore the process at your peril'.

This maxim could apply to all methods, including lectures, but it is certain that in using groups, it is not only ideas about the topic under discussion that are brought into play. The more participative the activity, the more people's *values, beliefs, concerns* and *evolving relationships* become part of the personal and collective experience.

It is also worth remembering that without *asking participants about their experience,* only a fraction of it is known to others, including the tutor. People make connections between what is happening in the session and other parts of their past or present experience and have different thoughts and feelings about the activity and the others involved in it. But they may not wish or feel able to make all of those thoughts public.

To demonstrate this, try the simple expedient of asking each person taking part in an activity to recall what was going through their minds at different points during the session. It can be most revealing, illustrating that the public conversation is often more to do with what people feel is expected of them than a reflection of their total experience. It is unfortunately all too common to hear trainers and teachers asserting what *they think* is going on in a group, or what they are *sure* participants are feeling, without confirmation from those involved.

Because, as we saw in the previous section, some of the group's process can be unconscious, it is useful to remember that *concerns about the immediate situation can 'leak' out as comments on more distant settings.* So for example, a conversation during a training programme about how difficult things are back at work, can mean that people are worrying about what it is going to be like for them here too.

## Making sense of it

*Different explanations can be applicable to the same event.* Two people finding it difficult to get on in a group simply might not like each other. On the other hand, they might represent ideological, gender or occupational differences which may involve others too. It might have something to do with the situation on the course or a relationship from work they have brought with them. Similarly, if someone is particularly quiet during a discussion, this may indicate a personal characteristic or, just as likely, a reflection on the climate which has developed in the group.

*No group can be fully understood without taking account of its context.* I mentioned earlier that how people behave in a group may be due to events before they arrived or to the relationships they bring with them. It can also reflect characteristics of the organization or social group they come from, whether competitive, caring, business-like, or ruthless. This idea is developed in the next chapter.

*Groups are microcosms of society* and what happens in them often reflects the same tensions, struggles and conflicting positions which are lived out day to day. The example of two people finding it hard to get on with each other I mentioned earlier may be best interpreted from a gender perspective if say, as woman and man, they are expressing ways or resisting acting in ways usually expected of them in society.

Some would say that too much emphasis can be put on the notion of 'the group', which is essentially a snapshot in time of contextual social and political processes: processes which are more complex in the example I have just given to be simply understood in terms of interpersonal affinity. The next three chapters develop this idea further.

## Doing something about it

As there can often be a number of things happening in a group during the same period and more than one plausible explanation, it can sometimes be difficult to know what to draw attention to.

A useful rule of thumb is to *be guided by what the purpose of the activity is.* There may be observations which would be of interest if the aim of the activity were to understand group behaviour, but if it is a project group in history or an 'action learning group' of managers in industry then the question to be asked is whether the group process is affecting the quality of what is being learnt.

Finally, it is worth noting that *doing nothing can often be the best response.* It is a useful rule to hold back from comment until what seems worth pointing out has happened on more than one occasion. This can help to avoid imposing your own preoccupations or biases on the group.

**Further reading**

I have included three sets of readings: theories of group behaviour I have referred to in this chapter, understanding group process, and adult learning. For the first two lists there are scores of possibles to choose from, many of which are influenced by psychodynamic theories if not specifically by Wilfred Bion's *Experiences in Groups* (1961). I have selected examples on the basis of accessibility as much as for the quality of the ideas contained in them.

*Theories of group behaviour*
'A social history of the 'T' group', by Stephen Potter in *Group Relations*, (1978) (see the note on GRTA which follows). *Interaction Process Analysis: a method for the study of small groups*, by R F Bales (1950); and for a broader discussion of theories which, like that of Bales and Tuckman, attempts to identify 'stages' which groups seem to go through, see 'Re-evaluating group development: a critique of the familiar models', by Marion McCollom. This is in the book she edited with Jonathon Gillette, *Groups in Context* (1990), in which they develop a perspective on group behaviour which draws on both open systems theory and group dynamics literature.

*Understanding group process*
*Small Groups and Personal Change*, edited by Peter B Smith (1980), has already been mentioned in Chapter 1. It contains chapters on different types of groupwork in different settings. The emphasis is not directly on educational settings as such but as learning and personal change are so closely related there is much of relevance to working with 'learning' groups.

Bion's ideas are essential reading for anyone using group methods but his writing can be hard going. There are two excellent summaries of Bion's ideas by other authors: 'The study of the small group in an organizational setting', by Barry W M Palmer in *Training in Small Groups*, edited by B Babington Smith and B A Farrell (1979) and 'The work of Wilfred Bion on groups', by Margaret J Rioch in *Group Relations Reader 1*, edited by Arthur D Colman and W Harold Bexton (1975).

*Adult learning*
*Pedagogy of the Oppressed*, by Paulo Freire, (1972); *Self-directed Learning: a guide for learners and teachers*, by Malcolm Knowles, (1975); and *Freedom to Learn*, by Carl Rogers (1969).

Finally, there are three associations worth knowing about as reliable sources of development for teachers or trainers intending to deepen their understanding of group process. The *Grubb Institute* puts on group conferences and conferences which are based on the psychology of group relations and systems thinking about organizations. Their address is Cloudesley Street, London N1 0HU.

The *Group Relations Training Association* is an informal affiliation of people interested in the application of groupwork in many different contexts including education, organizational development, social work, community work and clinical psychology. It is a good source of contacts, runs a conference and at least one T Group each year; there are also regionally based activities. Their administrator is Jill Brookes, Gala House, 3 Raglan Road, Edgbaston, Birmingham B5 7RA.

*National Training Laboratories*, now *NTL Institute for Applied Behavioral Science* carries out programmes of research and development towards the improvement of individual, group and organizational effectiveness: 1240 North Pitt Street, Suite 100, Alexandria, Virginia 22314-1403, USA.

# Introduction to Chapters 4, 5 and 6

In the first three chapters I have introduced ideas about the origins of groupwork, about the design of group methods for learning, and ideas which can be used to make sense of the complex processes involved in using groups.

As I explained in the Introduction, these are *some* of the ideas I have found useful and are included to illustrate the different perspectives teachers and trainers can draw on in designing and running group activities.

In the next three chapters, I use examples from practice to illustrate some ideas about learning groups which are important but which tend to be neglected: ideas which emphasize the importance of the social or organizational context and the ways that context is reflected in the internal life of the group.

# 4 Boundaries, Predictability and Control

## Introduction

There is always a purpose to any learning group activity. It may be quite specific, the aim being to illustrate or demonstrate an idea or theory. It can be to help in working together, as in so-called 'ice-breakers' for example, activities often intended to be on the lighter side to help people through the initial discomfort or strangeness of working in a different way or with people who are unfamiliar to them. Or the purpose may be more exploratory, intended to generate material for discussion around a chosen topic.

Whatever their purpose, a characteristic of group methods is that people's experience of them is more varied than the design on paper might suggest. So, as I summarized in Chapter 1, group activities involve participants in interactions with each other and with tutors or trainers in a different kind of working relationship than with other approaches. Connections will be made with past experience (see the first illustration below), or with the current organizational, social or personal context (an aspect covered in Chapter 5). Whatever the intended focus of the activity, the actual experience of it will be broader. What seems incidental to the tutor or trainer could be hugely significant to the student or trainee, more significant even, for educational or personal reasons, than the learning outcome intended.

In this chapter, I will develop these ideas about experiential learning using illustrations from different types of group activity. Specifically, I want to question the assumptions of *boundedness* and *predictability* often implicit in the way group methods are used. These assumptions are that, as with any other teaching method, it is clear when the activity starts and when it finishes and that the intended outcome should be predictable given the correct application of the design, particularly if the activity and discussion are *controlled* so as to keep to the purpose intended.

In order to explore these assumptions about boundedness and predictability, I will use illustrations from three kinds of group activity — a role play, an exercise and a game. The reason for choosing these three is that they are fairly typical of structured activities, and the more structured an event, the more it carries with it the assumption of predictability. Games, role plays and other experiential exercises of that kind, because they can seem quite simple in concept, lend themselves to the 'identify need — choose method — run — evaluate learning' model I discussed earlier. However, the point of this chapter is that experiential exercises are rarely that straightforward in practice. Outcomes of these methods are always more varied than the intended focus.

The three illustrations to follow each deal with a different aspect of the way people can experience group methods. The first illustration is concerned with the way participants will draw on past events of some significance to them, and the second with the consequences of a group activity for future learning relationships. The third illustration highlights the dilemma for anyone using group methods: that if there are likely to be unplanned and unforeseen consequences for participants, what are you supposed to do about that as tutor or trainer?

First though, a note on the term 'structure'. I am using it for convenience to discriminate roughly between different types of group-based activities. It is perhaps the commonest distinction made in practice and in the literature. Role plays are described as structured, and T groups or learning communities (which I will describe in Chapters 6 and 7) are commonly thought of as unstructured. Usually this is more or less the case, but not always. If structure is defined as aspects of method such as roles, rules and procedures, then a role play may be more or less structured depending how prescribed these aspects are. Some are very detailed in design and others much looser, allowing more discretion and interpretation to those taking part. It often seems to depend on the preferences of whoever is running the exercise and their beliefs as to whether structure helps learning or gets in the way.

On the other hand, someone running a T group may use more structured activities to help focus on particular dilemmas the group is encountering. But structure is not the only aspect of group methods which should be considered. The amount of direction also needs to be taken into account in terms of the ideas and explanations used. As illustrated in Chapter 1, it is possible in any type of event for a facilitator to leave roles, rules and procedures quite open but then to be highly prescriptive in drawing attention to some aspects of what unfolds and not others, or in choosing particular theories and ideas used to make sense of it all.

Strictly speaking, while the notion of 'structure' has its uses, it also has limitations as a yardstick for distinguishing between group exercises. It is much more reliable to add ideas such as 'direction' and 'control', to ask how much the structure and scope of an activity was predetermined and who it was determined by. An activity may come to be quite structured but in ways chosen jointly by staff and participants.

# Experiencing group methods

## ILLUSTRATION 1:
### Using role play to explore professional values – accessing the past

I first took part in this role play at a conference where it was demonstrated by the people who had developed it. I have used it since with teachers, managers, social workers and other course groups. It is nearly always warmly received, invariably good fun to take part in, easy to set up and serves well as a lead into discussion because of the issues it raises for participants.

**The role play**

*The purpose* of the role play is to explore the values which underlie professional practice. What sense of purpose do educators hold and what sense of right or wrong informs how they think and act?

The reason for using this particular role play is that it is designed to explore beliefs *contrary* to those participants hold as well as those on which they try to base their work.

*The situation.* Imagine the government has been overthrown and replaced by a right-wing junta. All professional groups will be asked to account for their practice. Psychologists (in this case, but it could be whichever professional group is involved in the role play) are required to attend a meeting of a review board which will decide whether their licence is to be renewed.

*The plan.* There are two groups: the review board in one and the psychologists in the other. The members of the review board are responsible for planning the rest of the session until the end of the role play. There is then a short break followed by a discussion of the exercise.

*Preparation* (30 minutes):

— the review board plan for the period up until the break, including their review, planning how they will conduct it and themselves during it, and decide on the questions they will ask the 'psychologists', bearing in mind the overall aims of the exercise.

— the 'psychologists' meet to prepare a justification for why they should be allowed to remain in practice under the new regime. They should begin by discussing what values they would like to think informed their practice but should also bear in mind the educational purpose of the exercise, and the role and responsibility given to the 'board' up until the break.

*How it went.* On this occasion — for it is never quite the same with every group — while the psychologists discussed their espoused values, the 'board' began enthusiastically laying out the room in as austere a setting as they could think of. They decided to take the stance that psychologists were only useful inasmuch as their work supported the state. The emphasis of their professional work should be for selection and control, for identification of subversives and their subsequent rehabilitation.

The psychologists were invited in as a group (there were about 12 of them) and seated in rows in front of the board (about eight in number) who were seated behind a long table. The board asked individuals one at a time to stand at the front and make a case for themselves. They were escorted to and from this position by security officials. During questioning, no other member of the psychologists' group would be permitted to speak, whether in support or in protest at the nature of the proceedings. The board, on the other hand, frequently talked over each other as they harangued the unfortunates brought before them.

This was all carried out in a stern and intimidating manner and, as often happens in role plays, the more 'in role' people became, the more realistic became the reactions of others. Carefully planned approaches by the psychologists aimed at compromise and appeasement gave way to impassioned defence of values participants held dear, as the result of aggressive and cynical questioning by board members. There were frequent outbursts of support from the floor which were quelled by security guards.

One dissenter refused to keep quiet. A tall, bearded pipe-smoker in his early 40s angrily attacked the board for their treatment of his colleagues, for their cynicism towards his learned and valued profession and for the ways they distorted and trivialized the thoughtful cases presented to them. He was repeatedly warned to keep quiet until his turn came but before long he would be up on his feet again, demanding a more just approach to the hearing. Finally, at the request of the board, he was forcibly ejected from the room by two officials, his pipe (accidentally) knocked to the floor and broken in the process.

**In the review**, this participant, still ashen-faced half an hour after the incident, described how only months earlier, as a political dissident in a country governed by a totalitarian regime, he had been summoned to a tribunal which had led to his being asked to leave the country. The approach adopted by the 'board' in this role play, while fairly far-fetched to most delegates, had for him been disquietingly similar to the treatment he had experienced. The attitude of the officials, the aggressive questioning, even the threatening presence of security guards, was painfully echoed at this conference session in the peaceful surroundings of an English college.

**Discussion**

Role plays have been used in psychotherapy since the 1920s. Educational applications of role play have been very varied, including training courses for probation officers, librarians and care-givers for the elderly, for developing communication skills in young people with visual impairment, for students of foreign policy, in social studies and in adult literacy programmes. The example I have used illustrates some typical features and some of the choices. There is a clear focus – in this case to explore professional values. It is involving and, although challenging, usually enjoyable to take part in. Most significantly, it enables a serious discussion of ideas in relation to participants' own ideas and experience.

But what this example illustrates is that to think of a role play as being a bounded exercise, with a specific focus applied to material generated in the 'here and now', underestimates the power of the method. After all, its antecedent, psychodrama, was used expressly to help people tap into past memories as well as into current concerns. In the same way, educational games can remind people of times at school when they felt clumsy, or when an emphasis on competitiveness left them feeling incompetent or alienated. *There is no way to be sure that methods as involving as these do not surface important associations from participants' past experience.* These associations may be pleasurable or painful and may, as with the dissident psychologist, be quite relevant to the focus of the exercise. But even if they are not, that makes them no less important to the individual concerned.

**ILLUSTRATION 2:**
**Using an exercise to explore difference in a group – future consequences**

In the same way that past experience may be drawn across the boundary of a structured exercise, so might its effects be carried over in time, long after the exercise is over. The exercise which I am using to illustrate this fact is a good example of an educational device which is ingenious, relatively simple to design or adapt but powerful in its capacity to generate material, learning and intensity among those taking part.

**The exercise**
At the beginning of a postgraduate programme for management teachers and trainers we had planned an early session for exploring the range of educational philosophies available to people working in this professional context. We were interested in grounding the discussion in the beliefs which course members held, taking account of the possibility of people's espoused views being at odds with their practice.

The exercise we chose was one in which group members are asked to form a line across the room between two 'poles', representing two different but recognizable sets of educational beliefs constructed so as to avoid, if at all possible, an implicit dichotomy of good practice – bad practice. These were on the lines of:

- whatever methods are used in education, it is important to provide sufficient structure to guide people's learning. Without it, they will be frustrated and confused and opportunity is wasted.
- structure in educational method of any kind will inhibit learning and there has to be room for the learners' own ideas and for them to decide on its direction and content. If not they will become frustrated and demotivated.

Course members were asked to discover their place in the 'line' by comparing their ideas with others, as far as possible on the basis of what they did, not what they liked to think they might do. So, exchanges hoped for would be of this kind:

| | |
|---|---|
| *First person:* | I think it's really important that students are encouraged to take responsibility for their learning. |
| *Second person:* | Do you mean as in planning their study time well and digging out literature with minimal guidance, or what? |
| *First person:* | Well yes, but not just that. I think we should let their ideas be just as influential as ours in what |

|              |                                                                                                                                                                                          |
| ------------ | ---------------------------------------------------------------------------------------------------------------------------------------------------------------------------------------- |
|              | they learn about and what conclusions they come to.                                                                                                                                      |
| *Second person:* | We should change places then. Whether I like it or not, I'm bound to a fairly strict curriculum. That's very different from what you've described which sounds much more student-centred. |
| *First person:* | Yes, I suppose you could say that.<br>*They change places.*                                                                                                                              |
| *Second person:* | Can I ask you something though? How often do your students get to write on your blackboard in class?                                                                                      |
| *First person:* | What do you mean? I often ask them to use the board so I can see if they've understood properly.                                                                                          |
| *Second person:* | Hmmm, maybe we should change back to where we were before!                                                                                                                               |

Using the 'line-up' as a device for looking at something as imprecise as beliefs about learning is quite difficult. Applying it to more factual or demographic details is less so. For example, it can be used to explore the association between class background and social values. The line can be formed on the basis of parents' or grandparents' occupational grouping and then related to current practices such as what kinds of school participants send their children to, do they use private or public health service, and so on. As with any experiential exercise, the hope is that limitations in the design will not detract from the discussion it is intended to stimulate.

So, on this occasion we introduced the method of forming a line on the basis of something tangible and, in the spirit of educational participation, invited ideas from the students on what this might be. Of all the ideas which could have been chosen, the group preference was for using *differences in income* as a relatively measurable item with which to demonstrate the method. It served its purpose in demonstrating the method well enough but a striking outcome for one of the tutors who also took part was the realization that some of the students earned two or three times his income. Nor had he appreciated before this exercise how much less he was paid than older colleagues doing exactly the same job. The feelings this generated lasted well into the rest of the week.

The line formed as the main exercise to reflect differences in educational values had repercussions which lasted even longer. The people who ended up at the extremes of the line became identifiable subgroups for the rest of the programme and were experienced by the other students as cliques.

An exercise to identify common ground may have been more constructive at this early stage in the course than one which 'heightened' difference.

## Discussion

As with the previous example, this one illustrates a number of points. For example, generating criteria from the student group for the introductory line-up was in keeping with the particular course philosophy. On the other hand, a staff-chosen example might have been less disruptive than comparing salaries. This exercise is also a good example of where an activity is easy to devise but possibly negative in consequence if misapplied or insensitively facilitated. It is *possible* to suggest a line which is to reflect differences of power or attractiveness amongst course group members. Possible, but inappropriate, unless certain understandings and expectations have already been developed within the group.

Most obvious is that 'boundedness' in experiential activities is an illusion of convenience. It is a convention in order to manage the time and structure of the session and the course. It is useful and important for everyone to be clear when the exercise is over, especially in role plays. There can be enough confusion in a group without adding to it by not knowing whether members are in role or out of it. *But ending the exercise does not necessarily end the experience or the thoughts and feelings generated by it.* At most they may be driven underground because of not seeming to fit within the formal focus of the session.

So, for example, groups who have taken part in exercises, business games, or project presentations and who have a sense of having won or lost – whether that was intended or not – carry their feelings into the subsequent discussion and even into later sessions. What have been characterized as 'fat and happy' or 'lean and hungry' groups can continue long after the activity which caused them is over.

## ILLUSTRATION 3:
### Using a business game to learn about management – unintended consequences: working with them or ignoring them

This example begins with a tutorial group for postgraduate management students during a discussion of the students' plans for their next seminar paper. Lucy, a young Danish student, was missing. She arrived 15 minutes or so into the session but was noticeably quiet and distracted. After a while she burst into tears, and sat for some time, head in hands, weeping quietly.

She was asked if anyone could help. Was it something she felt able to talk about? Was she worried about the paper? She said she did not want to talk about it, felt too distressed to say anything else and left. We were told later that she still seemed upset and was reported to have called her parents in Denmark quite frequently since the meeting. Apparently, the problem had arisen in another part of the programme.

Lucy was present at the next tutorial meeting two weeks later, her mood alternating between cheerfulness and anger. She was pleased to report she had found her topic for her paper, which was to be based on making sense of all that had happened to cause her such grief and which still made her angry to think about. She described what had happened.

As a student on an integrated management course Lucy had taken part in a business game used to consolidate and integrate learning from different parts of a programme in management studies. There were six competing groups in the game which took place in sessions spaced over a number of weeks. Preparation for these sessions was in each of the groups meeting without tutors. The game, like many business games, was based on selected models or systems developed in sales, marketing, financial control and so on. At the end, the teams were ranked in terms of the profit they had achieved and for the quality of the team presentations made to the whole class and the staff of the disciplines designed into the game. Lucy's team came last in the game and their presentation had not been rated very highly.

Worse was to come. At a debrief held by Lucy's team, she was criticized for her contribution to the exercise. From a distance, it seems as if, whether criticism of her was founded or not, she became a scapegoat for the team's failure. More than that, as Lucy reported it, she felt the object of attack as the other students expressed disfavour with her as a member of the group. Lucy was understandably distressed through all this, felt 'suicidal', called up the student counselling service and was only persuaded to stay on the course after long and repeated calls home to her parents. Her decision to write about this in a seminar paper for a course in educational innovations in management studies seemed appropriate, although it was difficult for her initially to achieve much objectivity in making sense of the whole affair.

### Discussion

It is easy, but probably harsh, to be critical of the staff in this particular incident. It would not be unusual for a student having a difficult time to find support from people outside the course in question. The staff responsible for the business game may never have come to know of the repercussions for one of their students, which lasted long after the exercise was over.

On the other hand the consequences for Lucy show how the outcomes of a group activity can be broader than the prescribed focus, can have effects long after the exercise has finished and may not be noticed or facilitated by the tutors or trainers. It might be argued that an activity of this kind, as likely as it is to generate quite intense social dynamics within and between groups, should have been used as much for making sense of those outcomes as well as for learning about its 'business' aspects. Fortunately, Lucy was able to reflect on what had happened through her written assignment.

# Experiencing group methods – a summary

The purpose of this chapter has been to emphasize the more unexpected consequences of group methods. The illustrations show how simplistic assumptions about the bounded nature of 'structured' activities lose sight of how different the outcome can turn out to be for participants.

The first illustration made the distinction between the *formalities* of an activity – when it starts and when it finishes and its intended focus – and informal, inevitable but often *hidden experience* of the students or trainees taking part. In this case the unplanned content arose through association with significant past events.

The second illustration showed how *consequences* of an activity could affect the learning relationships of those involved long after the exercise was over.

The third illustration emphasized the significance of these unlooked-for consequences of group activities: outcomes which were not intended but were nevertheless important to the individual and, potentially, *an added source of learning*.

A way of thinking about designing and running groups which takes account of unexpected consequences is shown in Figure 4.1.

The difference between what is *intended* through the design and what can be *experienced* from group methods in practice is not limited to activities which are more structured. The reason for basing this chapter on examples of structured exercises is that they are the ones which are more frequently planned and written about as though they were prescribable. A neat and bounded design for a group activity gives the impression that participants' experience is correspondingly neat and bounded. It is not usually like that. What is more, exerting more control in the discussion may enhance the *illusion* of tidiness, as participants cooperatively or dutifully keep within the bounds set by the tutor or trainer. This will determine the content of public discourse but it will not change private experience.

# Implications for tutors and trainers and the question of control

Whether unintended outcomes should be talked about in a learning group is a matter of judgement. Are they getting in the

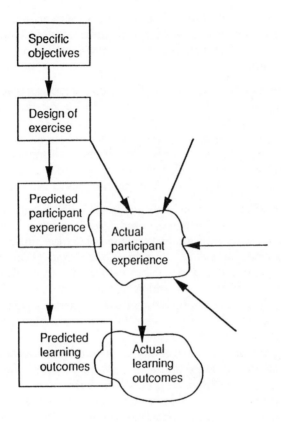

**Figure 4.1** *Design intentions and actual outcomes*
(Boot and Reynolds (1984), reprinted with the publisher's permission)

way of the primary purpose of the activity? Are they of sufficient significance to the participants concerned that they merit attention, whether relevant to the original purpose of the activity or not? Have they had such an effect on a member of the group that it would be negligent to ignore them?

This raises the question of who should decide whether this extra material is made public and, if so, how it should be dealt with. If it is the content of participants' experience then it seems right that they should have control over its use. It belongs to them. The point is that, as with any experiential approach, group methods are:

> ... not simply more efficient than conventional approaches, they are by their nature more intrusive into the personal and social world of the students. After all, they usually require students to reflect on their personal experience and to engage actively with each other. That is one reason for valuing such approaches, but it throws into greater relief the moral questions inherent in any tutor-student transaction. (Boot and Reynolds, 1983, p. 5).

The unpredictable richness of group activities means that using them in a cavalier fashion is ill-advised. There are hundreds of apparently 'simple' group tasks in the public domain, available to teachers and trainers in all subject areas and at all levels of education and training. They can be used as 'ice-breakers' at the start of a course or to add interest at any stage. But easy availability does not negate the need to understand the nature of this approach to learning and the processes they help bring about.

Being aware of the possibility of unpredictable outcomes does not mean that it is pointless to attempt a specific focus for a session or course based on groupwork. But it helps to remember that an intended focus will not limit participant experience. There is an argument for using structure to limit the uncertainty which people on courses have to contend with, although sometimes it seems that preoccupation with structure and control in the use of group methods has more to do with a tutor's discomfort than with their students'.

Given all this, it is advisable to leave adequate time for discussion in planning group activities, to allow for material which is peripheral but important to be worked with. It is also a responsibility of tutors and trainers to develop their understanding so as to be prepared for working with unpredicted events and material. These events may be pleasurable or, sometimes, as in the earlier illustrations, uncomfortable. Either way, with intelligent support, they can provide valuable understanding.

At the start of an adult education class in English literature, the tutor intended to develop the theme of novels as autobiographical. She began the first session by asking people to spend some time in small groups talking through their earliest memories of childhood. In one of the groups a middle-aged man broke down when his account reached a time in his childhood where he had been the object of serious bullying at school. This was unintended and unexpected, but the difference between his experience and that of Lucy's in the business game, was the sympathetic and skilful response of the tutor. Later, and on her advice, the student arranged for counselling which was the first step he had taken in dealing with this distressing episode in his early life.

**Further reading**

The ideas in this chapter owe much to the thinking which went into a paper written with Richard Boot, 'Issues of control in simulations and games' in *Simulation/Games for Learning* (1983b).

In a subsequent issue of the same journal there was a reply to this paper from Jeff Hearn (1983) entitled: 'Issues of control in simulations and games: a reconsideration', in which the author focused attention on the role and the power of the staff in the use of group activities.

# 5 Learning from the Milieu

So far I have illustrated the complexity of using group activities for learning, however apparently simple those activities may seem in design. I have also introduced the idea that whatever the intention behind the activity, the experience of people taking part is influenced by a number of sources, including the relationships that develop amongst group members. In this chapter I will develop these ideas further. The varied influences on the experience of group participants not only affect what they learn, or affect the relationships they carry forward into subsequent activities, they are a *source of learning* in their own right.

There is a long-standing interest in what people learn in education and training settings and a realization that learning is not limited to the content of the course alone, be it a language, a science or an applied subject such as social work or management. Students learn about what is expected of them in class directly from teachers and from each other, and more subtly through all the institutional paraphernalia of lecterns, high tables, desks in rows, horseshoes or circles, systems of rewards and punishment, and so on. These artefacts all convey prescriptions as to the role students and staff are to occupy during the educational process and the behaviour which is expected of them.

The same process happens through the use of group methods. The roles and relationships of staff and students, or trainers and trainees, are more varied because the methods are more varied. But, as with more conventional approaches, whatever the aim of the session, whatever it is intended people should learn from it, wider expectations and assumptions about the course and students' roles within it are likely to be conveyed through the design itself, its structures and the way the staff run the activity.

The illustrations in this chapter are chosen to show how the *design* of group methods transmits social values to the students or trainees taking part, sometimes in ways that contradict the educational values espoused by the tutors.

# Values and beliefs implicit in experiential learning

### ILLUSTRATION 1:
### Using 'ice-breakers' – expectations of the staff-student relationship

Imagine designing the first few days of a fairly participative programme for professionals from different organizations. If the course design is to work it is important that people are encouraged to 'loosen up' as soon as possible, to get to know each other and be prepared to join in the discussions which are to form the mainstay of the course method. But, realistically, people in the first few days will be restrained, shy or nervously outspoken, wondering who everyone else is and what it's going to be like spending time with them, excited or wishing they were somewhere else.

There is a wide range of introductory devices, or 'ice-breakers' as they are often called, to help people get through some of this natural restraint. Some might be familiar from other social settings, such as time to talk to one another about interests and background. Or there might be variations on this theme which are frequently used in training and education programmes, such as finding out about a classmate and then introducing them to the rest of the group. Or participants are invited to share with each other their hopes, fears, or reasons for choosing the course. Activities like these can be useful in accelerating the process of people feeling able to take part.

But there is more to it than that. For instance, whether the staff join in an activity or not could be an indication of expectations they have of their role and of the distance they feel appropriate between themselves and the participants. I worked closely with an industrial trainer for a number of years who would use activities like these to start up supervisor courses. But he always made it clear to course members on the first day that whatever hopes and fears they talked about in smaller, participant-only groups, how much of this they made public in the whole group subsequently was up to them. He wanted them to know from the start that his way of working would mean that they should always have control over what they made public and what they kept private. He could have suggested that the supervisors tell the whole group what came out of the initial introductions in twos or threes, but this would have given a different impression of where the balance of control lay.

There are other methods with the same intention that are even less like everyday ways of doing things. One that has been quite popular with trainers is the 'blind walk' in which, in pairs, one person is blindfolded and led by the other for a walk through the building or outdoors. As is often the case with these exercises, it is hard to know where they originated. It is one of a range probably spawned within the encounter group movement and intended as a device for focusing on an individual's comfort with leading, following, or on their difficulties with trusting others.

A blind walk can also be used as an ice-breaker early in courses. But what messages might this activity transmit about the course as a temporary institution? Something is certainly being signalled here by the staff about introducing techniques, unilaterally, which cut across the conventions of everyday life. And there is a whiff of humanistic paternalism about the trust which it is implied the students will have to be prepared to place in the tutors if exercises like this are to be sprung on them from time to time. And what if exercises like this one are used with groups of students from different cultures, some of which may have different and quite strict views governing relationships between staff and students, or between men and women? Believing that respect should be shown to tutors is likely to inhibit protest against an activity which breaches other conventions students value. So they will go along with it.

Apparently, a signal has been given that respect for cultural difference might not be high on the staff team's agenda. I stress 'apparently', because in my experience respect probably is high on the agenda but no-one has noticed the contradictory message implicit in using this type of exercise.

## Discussion

As well as what participants learn about the educational and social aspects of the course through their experience of the methods and processes introduced by the staff, they also pick up cues from which they learn more generally about citizenship, about values and attitudes they are expected to take as members of organizations, of occupational or professional groups, or of society. This area of interest is well documented in writings of educationalists and sociologists.

For example, cartoons at the top of pages in a mathematics book might be included to make it visually more appealing and therefore more inviting to the young reader. But they may also serve to reinforce the different roles expected of girls and boys, the little boys caricatured as rough and tough in their denim dungarees, and the little girls in gingham frocks and pigtails suitably charming, exuding innocence. This is disconfirming at some level of consciousness for little boys who are disinclined to be rough and tough and for little girls who want to be. Many language textbooks have similar features: illustrative cartoons reinforcing the role stereotypes expected of men and women.

These are obvious examples of the subtle or indirect ways that written texts transmit more than the subject ideas they are intended to convey. It can be more complex than that. Basil Bernstein (1971) has developed the idea that the way subjects are structured in school curricula, with some seen as more central than others, subtly yet insidiously introduces or reinforces notions of division and hierarchy to pupils at an early stage in their social development.

## Summary so far

It is not my intention here to cover these ideas in any detail, and I have added some references to writings which do. The points I have been making are these:

- more than course content is conveyed in educational settings;
- indications of the roles and relationships expected within the course may be transmitted implicitly through staff practices;
- wider expectations of social attitudes and behaviour may also be conveyed through the medium of the course and its methods.

In the next section I will focus on the particular way all this applies to group methods.

# Group activities as a medium for social values

An idea I have found useful is what Malcolm Parlett and others (1977) call the 'learning milieu'. It provides an alternative way of thinking about the learning setting, methods and relationships than merely as background, a means to an end, a sort of scaffolding with no other significance than to make the intended learning possible. The idea of the learning milieu, or as others have described it, the 'learning environment', acknowledges the complicated web of events within which each participant studies and learns. Parlett and colleagues described it in this way with schools in mind, but the idea is just as apt for all educational settings:

> [The learning milieu] is the social-psychological and material environment in which students and teachers work together. The learning milieu represents a nexus or network of cultural, social, institutional and psychological variables. These interact in complicated ways to produce, in each class or course, a unique pattern of circumstances, pressures, customs, opinions and work-styles which suffuse the teaching and learning that occur there. The configuration of the learning milieu, in any particular classroom, depends on the interplay of numerous different factors. For instance, there are numerous constraints (legal, administrative, occupational, architectural and financial) on the organization of teaching in schools; there are pervasive operating

assumptions (about the arrangement of subjects, curricula, teaching methods and students' evaluation) held by faculty; there are individual teacher's characteristics (teaching style, experience, professional orientation and private goals); and there are student perspectives and preoccupations (Parlett and Hamilton, 1977).

This underlines the possibility that we might learn a lot more from a course or a session than the curriculum as discharged by the teacher or trainer. Instead of thinking: 'This is a geography class using the lecture, or case study, or a simulation as the method. How effective is the method in enabling people to learn about geography?', we could ask: 'What is being learned here, *including* ideas about geography?'

The notion of the learning milieu is perhaps best elaborated through an illustration using a 'simple' experiential exercise to compare the intended focus or aims of the exercise with the possible 'milieu' which emerges through its use and is experienced by the students. It develops the idea introduced in the previous chapter which described how the outcome in the experience of the participant is likely to be broader than the tutor's intent (see Figure 4.1 in Chapter 4); that what stands out for a participant may or may not be what the session was designed for. After that I will say why I think the possibility of learning from the milieu is especially significant when the approach is based on groupwork of some kind.

## ILLUSTRATION 2:
### An exercise to demonstrate the role of influence in interpersonal communication – learning from the course milieu.

This is another of those exercises which, on the face of it, seem very straightforward; so much so that I have often used it to demonstrate to teachers and trainers how different in practice experiential exercises can be from design intentions. I – or someone else – would run the exercise then invite everyone, including me, to say what they remember going through their minds during the session. I am always struck by how much more is going on than was apparent at the time. The account which follows is loosely based on the same approach. What I imagine the students might have said is drawn from several occasions.

**The exercise**

*The purpose* of the exercise was to look at a specific aspect of interpersonal communications: the different ways people get someone's attention and keep it. A second aim was for the participants, a group of 15 students on a social-work course, to reflect on their own ways of doing this and how they could do it better.

*The session.* First, there is an introduction of ten minutes or so by the tutor, of basic ideas about the role of power and influence in conversations between more than two people and how non-verbal communication plays its part in this. There then follows the exercise. Three students volunteer to take part, the rest observe. The three are Gary, Jonathan and Sophie. Three chairs are arranged in a line, so the effect is like sitting beside people in an airplane. Sophie is in the middle of the two men. For 15 minutes Gary and Jonathan have to engage Sophie's attention any way they can.

To end, people say what they observed and there is a discussion about the methods used to gain and hold attention and the sort of relationships which seemed to develop through this.

*How it went.* The session started ten minutes late – Alan, the tutor, had been waylaid by his head of department about timetabling problems with the following term. He introduced the session and answered a few questions, mostly about the exercise itself. The exercise was lively, with the two men trying various ways to get Sophie's attention: finding new and interesting topics, raising their voices, gesticulating, sleeve-pulling and so on. It ran over time and was followed by a discussion of observations with the tutor rounding off with some models explaining the dynamics of interpersonal communication, and their application to professional settings such as meetings or interviews.

*What the tutor thought about the session:*

> It seemed to go well enough. I was a bit rushed because of being delayed, but they're a tolerant bunch and I've run this so many times and it always goes well. There was the usual range of

possibilities and a good discussion. They seemed to get something out of it and that's what matters.

*What the students thought:*

I remember thinking I'd never really thought that much about how I talk to people. I'll be watching myself more from now on.

I was a bit fed up he was late again. We know his department has problems but we're the ones who suffer.

I didn't like the way Gary kept putting his hand on my arm. It reminded me of being touched up by men in bars. I suppose it's all relevant but that spoiled it for me.

I was interested in the exercise but his ideas about communication are a bit limited. OK as far as it goes, but a bit mechanistic. I was wondering what this has to do with the huge social problems we're going to have to grapple with when we're back in the real world.

I was glad I didn't have to do the role play. I find Jonathan a real pain. We'd have argued all the time and spoiled it for everyone else.

When Alan introduced the session I thought 'Oh no, not this stuff again'. We've often asked him to do less of these Mickey Mouse games. He asks what we want and we tell him, but it doesn't make any difference. We know the other course tutors think it's a waste of time too.

It made me remember times when I was younger and felt left out of things. Really embarrassing some of them. I wish I'd done something like this when I was at school.

## Discussion

The aims and method were straightforward enough – the outcome richer; certainly more varied than the tutor's design intended. The students' experience consists of *educational* aspects: associations with past experience or relevance to the future, even someone thinking it was a role play, which it was not; thoughts about *pre-existing and changing relationships* with classmates; *attitudes of other staff* towards this part of the course; *administrative pressures* affecting the tutor and, through him, the students; even *philosophical issues* – what is the 'real world' and who defines it as such?

All of these make up the learning milieu. The point to develop from this idea is this: if participants' experience is anything like as varied as this, who is to say which of it all has most effect on them? Do they learn only from the content of the course? Is it possible that we can learn from *any* aspect of the milieu? Of all that suffuses people's experience of the course or training event, some aspects may affect how much or how easily they learn but they may also provide a source of learning.

# The medium of groupwork as a source of learning

Even with conventional methods such as lectures it is clear that more goes on in the minds of students than the lecturer is aware of and that more is involved than simply taking in information (Hodgson, 1984). But group activities are particularly significant for these reasons:

- The way the activity is designed and organized reflects similar principles on which organizations and the wider social context are based. There is a sense in which the group is society in microcosm. The basis of power and influence, the way choices are arrived at, the norms of behaviour which emerge, the ways in which conflicts of interest are worked with; all these aspects of living and working in society and the tensions and dilemmas they pose, are recreated in groups designed for learning.
- In designing group activities, there is the choice of the full range of social or political versions which people encounter day-to-day at work and in the community. Group methods can be designed on the basis of hierarchical, democratic or collective principles.
- Whether we are intending to or not, the way we put an activity together emphasizes a particular version of the way things get done in society. If one model predominates, then the principles it is based on are reinforced by our choice of approach to group-based learning.

I believe these possibilities are of special significance to teachers and trainers who are using groups in their work as a way of encouraging more democratic ways of working. Using groups does not of itself necessarily achieve this. Group activities can reflect democratic principles or they can celebrate hierarchy. If they are used merely to add interest or to 'motivate' participants, then to people who work out of that reasoning, the ideas in this chapter may not count for much. But if group methods are intended to enable people to understand and work within more participative structures, then the form they take matters.

So, for example, in the illustration of the communications exercise, likes and dislikes between students could simply be accepted as background, or they could be something to learn from. Tensions within the department which affect the tutor's punctuality could be merely a source of irritation which gets in the way of the work the session was intended for, or it could be how students learn about their relative status within the institution. Seeing how little notice is paid to their ideas, even when they have been invited to give them, could have a wider significance. This could be how they learn a model of authority they will meet in many organizations when their education is over.

The illustrations have shown how methods used with learning groups *transmit social and educational values* to the students who take part in them. The four illustrations to follow develop this idea by focusing on the *models of organization* and working relationships implicit in the design. The first of these is in an educational context and the second is of an in-house training programme for industrial supervisors. The last two illustrations show how the *dominant culture* of an organization or profession is reinforced through the medium of a training programme using experiential methods.

### ILLUSTRATION 3:
### A revision 'quiz'.

**The design**
During a course, or near its end, it can be useful to have a session for revision. Here is an approach based on working in groups

which students enjoy and seems useful to them. It is appropriate to many subjects and can provide an interesting way of consolidating and sharing what has been learned, or of identifying topics or ideas which have not been understood clearly.

The students are divided into an even number of teams so as to get a good mix on the basis of performance during the year. Each team has 20 minutes or so to prepare questions which it will put to one of the other teams based on the course content. There are two rounds, so that everyone has the opportunity to ask questions and to answer questions put to them.

*Rules.* There is no access to notes or books during question design or during the quiz; marks out of five are decided by the questioning team, depending how they judge the quality of the answer. If the answer is wrong, the team that put the question needs to show they had a satisfactory answer or they incur a penalty; the tutor is the final arbiter in cases of doubt.

## Discussion

Someone opening the door on this session would think how lively it was, how engaging. People shouting over each other, laughing, groups huddled together conspiratorially. Then the quiz, earnest consultation, delight when an answer is known and accepted, dismay and challenge when it is pronounced 'wrong'. A traditional educationalist might worry about where the teacher was in all this: is there one in the room even? It seems anarchic. The teacher only speaks for five minutes or so at the outset and the classroom becomes a hive of activity for the rest of the session.

But where did the direction come from? Who is in the driving seat? More specifically, where have the various choices that make up this session been made?

If the decisions made in the design and running of this session were plotted in terms of staff or student origin it would look like this:

| DECISIONS | ORIGIN |
|---|---|
| Choice of exercise | Tutor |
| Timing during course | Tutor |
| Location | Tutor |
| Time allocated | Tutor |
| Room layout | Tutor |
| Team composition | Tutor |
| Plan for the session | Tutor |
| Tutor's role as arbiter/timekeeper | Tutor |
| Questions/answers | Students |
| The curriculum it's all based on | Tutor (exam board) |

So clearly there is a distinction to be made between being active, which this is, and being participative, which it is only in part. The illusion of activity is even more pronounced in role plays, games and simulations where there may be a dramatic or physical element. They can be good fun and instructive, but being busy, however enjoyably, isn't at the same level of taking part that a more participative approach would entail. As training for democracy, if a whole course were to be put together on these lines, something would be missing. There is the illusion of taking part but in reality this is partial and in terms of opportunity to influence the decisions which shape the direction and content of the event, quite limited.

That is not to deny that this can be a useful method to use to stimulate revision, although there are more choices in this design which could be shared with, or made by, the students, short of the ultimate step of relaxing hold of the curriculum.

But if all the design decisions in a course based on group methods were as weighted to the tutor as in this example, however active the sessions seemed, the organizational principles transmitted through the medium of design would be far from democratic. This can happen in courses that are designed with the express intention of encouraging participation, as the next example illustrates.

## ILLUSTRATION 4:
### A programme in consulting skills – developing subordination

At an early stage in my career I worked as a consultant with a management development team in an industrial organization. One of our projects was to design and run a series of programmes to develop consulting skills in junior and middle management. This was because, as part of a shift in practice to a more participative management style, there was more organizational development (OD) activity in progress than the consultants and trainers could cope with. Others were needed to work part-time in assisting in the usual types of OD activity: team-building; facilitating meetings, working parties and project teams; providing counselling or consulting support to line managers.

The staff team for this project were two of the company's management developers, and two consultants. The design for the programme was to be a one-week residential course and nine follow-up days at monthly intervals. The course was to be heavily based on experiential exercises using groups. This echoed the emphasis in the company on delegation and team-work and would provide a way of developing course participants' understanding of group and intergroup processes. It also meant there would be plenty of practice in counselling and problem-solving consulting, hence the overall title of 'consulting skills'.

The problem was that the follow-up sessions were a disappointment. Given the participative culture espoused by senior management and the added responsibility which the course members would be taking on, it seemed a good idea that they should be given responsibility for planning and organizing these follow-up days. This was not a success. They seemed lost, unsure as to what agenda to set for these sessions, frustrated at being left to cope with this on their own and had to be helped out by the staff team. This was disappointing when the residential weeks had seemed to go so well, with a very positive response from the same participants who were now finding everything so difficult. It was especially disappointing when what seemed lacking was an ability to exercise more discretion or to take more initiative, abilities at the heart of the changes the course was supposed to help bring about.

**Discussion**

We decided that the problem was in the design of the residential weeks. We had made the mistaken assumption that an experiential programme, with an emphasis on group activities, would reinforce the teamwork being increasingly encouraged at all levels of the organization. But as in the earlier example of the revision quiz, this logic was superficial and its assumptions not borne out in practice. Certainly the week was very involving and the course members active, more so than in most of the training they had received before this programme.

On closer examination however, it was equally clear that the staff team's approach to the week, while involving, had been very directive. The planning and design for the sessions, the models and frameworks used to make sense of group activities, consulting and counselling approaches, were all chosen or devised by the staff team. The course members' role was limited to contributing their experience and observations within this framework.

Participants' contributions had been significant but given the purpose of the project, almost totally lacking in the area of choosing, decision making, or having influence over the structures and methods of the week. This would have been good practice for planning the follow-ups or for the new role they were being trained for. In effect they had an enjoyable time working within the structures the staff team had chosen for them. Unintentionally, we had undermined the development we believed we were helping to bring about.

## ILLUSTRATION 5:
### Training as reflection of the organization's culture

In another project, in a different company and working this time with a colleague as participant researchers studying course members' experience of a supervisory training programme, we were struck by the parallels between the ethos of the programme and the way the supervisors described the dominant management style within the company.

Managers apparently espoused a participative way of working with their staff, expressing an interest in supervisors taking more responsibility, more initiative and being more involved in day-to-day decisions. In practice, the supervisors did not see it working this way at all. For the most part they felt left out of management decisions and rarely consulted.

What interested us, and the course staff responsible for the programme, was that the supervisors' experience of the course was very similar to their experience of management, as their comments to us at the time indicate:

*About work:*

> If I have a problem, I have no authority to deal with it. I have to put it to the manager ... it's all very well them saying *how* we should work, but it doesn't work. We are not involved in management.
> ... so supervision doesn't count, they undermine supervisors and make us look fools.
> ... we're not responsible enough ... as they [management] say, a little knowledge is dangerous. But we're not involved at all.

*About the course:*

> Yes, he [a tutor] seemed to override the people who talked. Yet we'd been told we could. He didn't allow the audience to participate ... to speak a bit more.
> We'd get a lot of answers. They'd learnt their methods and they weren't going to break them.
> He wouldn't let you get involved. There wasn't much chance to get involved.

## Discussion

Interestingly, the supervisors did not seem aware of the connection between the way they experienced higher management at work and the way they experienced trainers during the course, although they were critical of how their contributions were being thwarted in both settings. It seemed that unintentionally the training staff, again using group and experiential methods for the most part, were reinforcing supervisors' expectations of their role at work by replicating the illusion of involvement during the course: involvement promised but not often delivered.

In this illustration the way the trainers had worked with course members had sometimes been closer to senior management practice than to their own educational aims. But the messages teachers or trainers transmit through the medium of their educational method are not necessarily monochromic. The context may represent a mixture of different, perhaps conflicting value systems and these may be reflected in the course milieu, as the final illustration shows.

## ILLUSTRATION 6:
### A research methods programme – contrasting values within the learning milieu

Another project we carried out was the evaluation of a course in research methods for management teachers (Hodgson and Reynolds, 1980). The staff were university academics but they shared an interest in using participative methods: group discussions based on course members' work or case studies and an opportunity for participants to choose the topics for more formal sessions.

As in the evaluation project with the supervisors, we based our approach on finding out as much as we could about how participants had *experienced* the programme. We were struck by the way their experience of the course was from two different perspectives. One seemed to reflect their consciousness of the *research ethos* they belonged to – or hoped to belong to. The other had more to do with the *educational philosophy* reflected in the design and methods used during the course. These seemed based on dissimilar values with participants experiencing the tutors as the source of both of them:

> The tutor was very dogmatic in the way he discussed each person's project. He had done this from the point of view of how he saw research should be done and consequently there had been little interaction between group members.
>
> The case study was valuable in providing new insights from which I could look at my own research. I began to feel vulnerable if this was to be the standard of criticism of my research by others.

Contrast these statements with the ones which follow:

> On the whole it was most interesting. But it meant going out of one's way to make one's own experience interesting and rewarding. One could not rely on any structured, organized planning approach to provide these opportunities ... it was a matter of wanting to learn and grabbing or creating the opportunities to be grabbed.
>
> I liked the tone of the discussion – relaxed, friendly, supportive. Though there may have been an element of 'let's be kind to one another, because we're all vulnerable aren't we?'

The first statements, and others like them, were about how it felt to be part of the research community, with its rigorous standards, the academic tradition of sitting at the feet of elders and of subjecting work to criticism of such severity as to put self-esteem at risk – a baptism of fire in order to enter a privileged community of scholars.

The other statements reflect a different milieu altogether of support, collaboration and self-directed learning, where one's own and one's colleagues' ideas are valued as much as those of the tutors – a milieu more associated with participative approaches than traditional methods.

## Discussion

At the time we described what we felt were contradictory elements of the learning milieu on this programme as follows:

> Fundamental to the research profession and maintained by its procedures of supervision and accreditation, is the principle of hierarchy based on expert authority. In contrast to this, participative approaches to learning depend on validation of ideas, or choice of direction being shared among students and teachers alike. The more participative a course, the more it contrasts with the model of authority dominant in the research community for, as the course director reflected during the week, a programme in research methodology does usually ... 'reflect the research culture where more senior people feel they have the right to pontificate and be listened to'.

Sometimes aware of the implications of this contradiction, participants wondered if it would undermine the opportunity the course was meant to provide:

> Possibly we didn't know each other's work well enough to start offering penetrating criticism, thereby preserving self-esteem, but losing out on feedback which would have increased the learning of the exchange.

All this should not mean that implicit contradictions in methods and approach have to be ironed out in some way. It is worth being aware of the messages it is hoped might be transmitted, including any contradictions contained in them and whether this is what is happening in practice, as between values of a 'caring profession' and its predominant management practices, for example. Both these elements may be part of the learning milieu within a course for hospital workers or for the staff of a children's home. It may be useful to identify contradictions as a way of learning more about the organizational or professional tensions they reflect. I will develop this idea in the next chapter.

## Summary

The previous chapter illustrated how the simplest design for group activity will probably be more complex than that in outcome, and that influences and effects pass easily across the boundary between the activity and its context, an idea I hope to develop later.

In this chapter my intention has been to show how the structure and process of group activities, based as they are on social and organizational principles, may transmit those principles to the people taking part, as well as provide them with an interesting and enjoyable means of exploring topics of one kind or another.

I have also made much of the difference between keeping students busy and providing them with an opportunity to take part in the more significant, democratic sense. Without wishing to, group activities might *seem* to encourage participation but can actually constrain it, if decisions about content and process are mostly determined by the staff.

In the next chapter, I will describe some more open, less

directed group methods, more difficult to run perhaps than the examples I have used so far, but with more significant opportunity for participation.

## Further reading

'Learning from lectures', by Vivien Hodgson (1984) explores students' experience of lectures and its influence on their learning. This chapter is in *The Experience of Learning* edited by F Marton, D Hounsell and N Entwistle, a collection of papers by authors who share an interest in understanding educational process through the experience of students.

A paper which develops the idea of the milieu, including teaching method, as a source of learning is 'Learning the ropes', (Reynolds, 1982) in which I drew on a number of illustrations from education and training. Two further papers are based on the research with Vivien Hodgson described in the fifth and sixth illustrations in this chapter; these are: 'The hidden experience of learning events: illusions of involvement', (Hodgson and Reynolds, 1981), and 'Participants' experience as the basis of course improvement' (Hodgson and Reynolds, 1980).

# 6 Groups as Open Systems

## Introduction

In the two previous chapters I have emphasized that the boundaries of groups are precise only in terms of design; in practice they are quite open. Whatever a group activity is set up for, however definite its focus, its intended material, or its start and its finish, people's experience of the past or of the current context will be drawn into it, as will their hopes or concerns for the future.

As a result of the activity, there may be changes in the context too. Relationships and understandings can change through experiential methods, which is why they are used as part of training programmes in organizations, as for example the way in which team development is used (see next chapter).

In this chapter, these ideas are developed in relation to two themes:

- First, that the internal dynamics of a group also reflect social processes arising from its organizational or cultural context.
- Second, that it may be necessary to take account of these wider social processes in helping participants make sense of their experience of learning in groups.

In other words, groups of all kinds, regardless of purpose, are not detached or dislocated from their social context. The attitudes, beliefs and preferred ways of working which people bring with them into a learning group are likely to be the same as those developed and expressed in their day-to-day lives. The differences in ways of relating to others due to class, gender, race or culture are not left at the threshold when people join a group. In this sense the group is best seen as a microcosm of the society from which it is drawn.

# Taking account of the context

Although I stressed in an earlier chapter that the differences between lecturing and group methods are often oversimplified, it seems obvious that group methods are more likely to support expression of these social influences in a way that lectures do not. A lecture is what it is: a useful device for helping people learn, usually with relatively straightforward expectations of the role of lecturer and audience. Whatever thoughts, feelings and associations go on in the listeners' minds *will* be coloured by social or cultural factors too, but for the most part, in a lecture, all those processes are hidden from the view of others.

In group activities, however, the more interaction there is between participants, the more social values and beliefs are expressed and, as I have illustrated in previous chapters, the more they form part of the experience of those present. For this reason, the illustrations I will use in this chapter are from more 'open' designs of learning groups – that is to say, designs where there is a clear purpose to the activity but with minimal direction or structure introduced by whoever is running them. Designs of this type are likely to involve considerable interaction between group members, not only in exchanging ideas but in making decisions, planning and making choices with others.

The purpose of more open methods might be to develop an understanding of groups as such, as with T groups or group conferences. Or, as in the 'learning community' approach (see Chapter 7), it might be to provide a more participative approach to learning in any subject area. In either case, the degree of student or trainee involvement means that it is essential for tutors to understand and work with the social processes which emerge if they are to help participants make sense of their experience.

So, for the tutor or trainer, there will be a question of how much of what is happening in a group reflects its context. Should group processes which are contextually significant be passed over as peripheral to the aims of the activity, or should they be worked with in some way? If they need to be worked with, is the appropriate level of interpretation interpersonal – because whatever occurred was between individuals, or social – because what occurred reflects the social or cultural context? And, in the same way, is the appropriate way of making sense of whatever has occurred in the group to be from an interpersonal or socio-political perspective, or both?

These are complex questions and I am conscious of how much thinking has gone into understanding them. For example, the work of people such as Trist, Miller and Rice at the Tavistock Institute of Human Relations has been very influential in developing ideas about boundaries and the relationship between different parts of any social system (see, for example, Rice, 1971). The title I chose for this chapter is an acknowledgement of their contribution and the development of the field of socio-technical systems which has followed in their wake. Also relevant here is the work of more critical social theorists who warn of the limitations of thinking of groups as discrete entities, separating them in some way from their social context and, in so doing, obscuring the political processes of class, gender or race of which they consist.

I cannot hope to do justice to these ideas here. But, without oversimplifying the issues involved, I hope the illustrations which follow show how contextual processes are relevant to learning groups. In understanding experiential groupwork, there is no substitute for 'doing it', but this chapter and the suggested readings at the end of it are intended as a contribution to making sense in practice of the complex interrelationships between groups and their context.

## ILLUSTRATION 1:
### An intergroup exercise – crossing boundaries

The connections between group activities and their context can be amusing as well as telling. An extramural department of a university had asked for an intergroup event to be run for trade union officials attending a weekend course in economics, industrial relations and what was called in those days 'behavioural science'. The aim of the event was to study behaviour between groups. The task of the groups that took part was described as being: 'to learn about what happens within and between groups by being in one'. The overall purpose of using this exercise was to examine the issues of authority, conflict and representation fundamental to the role of union officials.

During the course of the event, which lasted a whole Saturday, one of the participants, on the way to the toilets, passed by the open door of a lounge in the college we were using for the course just as the Manchester United footballer, George Best, was ordered off the field for throwing mud at the referee. The participant wrote this episode on a scrap of paper and once back in the event started its circulation round the groups.

This changed the course of the exercise as the groups which received the note set about decoding this mysterious but, they presumed, significant piece of information. It was assumed that the note had been injected into the exercise by the staff to enable them to research participants' reactions to it. All this came to light in the final plenary session and parallels were readily drawn with processes of rumour and myth-making which clutter negotiations in the workplace.

**Discussion**
The televised incident on the soccer field was not the only intruder in this intergroup event. The ease with which participants assumed that this diversion had been instigated by the tutors indicated, among other things, their perception of the tutors as members of a profession who habitually get up to all sorts of tricks in order to study the reactions of unwitting subjects. This intergroup dynamic between the participants and the tutors was as much born of societal assumptions people brought with them to the exercise as anything which emerged from it on the day.

In an earlier chapter I mentioned how talk in a group about the world outside the event could actually indicate concerns or hopes of group members for the activity they are involved in here and now. The reverse can also be the case. A good deal can be learned about people's immediate context by what happens when they meet to work together experientially in a group. The next illustration and the one that follows it show how the organizational, professional or social context can be revealed through the medium of a group activity and how this can be of use.

## ILLUSTRATION 2:
### An organization simulation – finding out about the organizational ethos.

An interesting way, experientially, to learn about organizing, managing or coordinating work effort, is to set up a temporary organization with the course participants. The activity described in this illustration, a simulation of a kind, is a rather more elaborate version of the 'Designing tasks for others' exercise described in Chapter 3. With various colleagues I have used it with a wide range of students and training course participants: social work students; school teachers; community workers; probation officers; management students and professionals in various kinds of organizations. In this case the participants were local government officers who worked for the same authority.

*The purpose* was described as an opportunity to explore in practice the effects and problems (individual, group or intergroup) of working within a task organization.

*The plan.* The exercise, which usually lasts for three or four hours, but could be longer, begins with informing the participants of the following givens:

*The organization*
Initially there will be two groups:
- the design group
- the task group.

*The design group*
– the choice of structure, roles and procedures for the organization is the design group's responsibility (whether hierarchical, consultative, democratic or collective);
– this group is responsible for the design of the task or tasks carried out within the organization. These tasks should be intended to develop understanding of the social and political aspects of work or organizations.

*The task group*
— share ideas about the form of organization they would normally prefer and their beliefs and values concerning working relationships;
— carry out whatever tasks have been designed for them.
At the outset, each group should choose a participant observer.

Some additional points would usually be made: the role of the staff is to clarify the givens if need be, to observe, to comment on any group process if it seemed useful to the participants at the time, and to lead the review later. It would be stressed that the exercise was not a role play nor was it intended as a way of demonstrating the tutors' view of one organizational model as superior to others.

*What happened.* The participants were 16 local government officers. The two groups formed quite quickly and moved to separate rooms to discuss their responsibilities and preferences for how to work both within their own group and with the other group. The design group favoured an organization in which, as 'management', they would be consultative, supportive, choosing a task for the other group to carry out unsupervised, so allowing them as much discretion as possible in determining the detail of the task. The task chosen would be one which would help the task group develop their understanding and skills of team work.

While all this was being worked out in the design group, the task group spent a rather desultory half hour reflecting on the pointlessness of stating their preferences for the sort of organization they would like to work in. They thought it inevitable that this would be determined for them by the other group. They made no attempt to contact the design group, resignedly accepting the staff member's observation that this was self-fulfilling and likely to ensure the lack of influence they were afraid of.

Eventually, a representative of the design team made an appearance and was politely, if unenthusiastically, received. The task she brought to them was as follows:

As our borough has tourist potential which is not being realized, the design group would like you to spend the next two hours designing and conducting a survey of people's opinion of the town's amenities. Try if you can to canvass visitors as well as citizens. Leave time for a presentation of your findings to the management team.

This appealed to the task group who set about designing a survey with vigour, occasionally visiting the 'management' group for clarification and to report progress. After a while, the task group members could be seen leaving the training block, clipboards and raincoats at the ready, moving in the direction of the town's main street which was close by. The design group, pleased that their idea had been taken up so readily, relaxed, drank tea and started to plan for the presentation.

Some time later, in ones and twos the survey team began to reappear and could be found busily working with the data and preparing their report. The presentation went well and the management team were pleased with the information which they believed would prove a useful pilot for a real exercise of this type in the future. Everyone seemed to have enjoyed it.

The review began with a confession from the task group that those data had not been collected at all. They had indeed left the building, only to return immediately through a side entrance to begin concocting spurious results in the warmth and comfort of their room. This charade was repeated later as they 'returned' from carrying out the survey. Some of the design team were shocked. Some felt foolish, recalling their earlier enthusiasm and some were amused. Others felt hurt and let down by the deception.

There was much to be discussed after this. But observations on the detail of how the groups had worked amongst themselves and with each other seemed less important than the element of deceit and the different feelings which that had aroused. Not surprisingly these were still evident well after the organization simulation had ended and into the review, illustrating the distinction between what is planned and what is experienced, as discussed in an earlier chapter.

Most significant, as one of the officers pointed out, was that this behaviour had caricatured one of the ways they normally worked with each other across departmental boundaries. There was sometimes an element of pretence in reporting on work carried out as requested, instead of expressing reservation or criticism with what was being asked. Everyone knew this happened and that nothing was ever said – until now – to create a more honest way of dealing with each other. There was agreement that this was the case and that without intending to, the task group had reflected this aspect of work in an exaggerated way through the medium of the exercise.

## Discussion

One of the strengths of this exercise is that different organizational forms can emerge. Participants experiment with structures they prefer but do not usually encounter, or recreate the one they currently work within in order to explore its limitations, or to understand familiar problems of communications, conflict, delegation, difficulties of representation, of working across group boundaries and so on.

But it also seems that because of its open structure, the exercise can provide a canvas on which participants express not only their individual values and beliefs, but those which characterize their organization when, as in the case of these local government officers, all participants come from the same workplace.

There is a practical value in the way the context can be expressed through the application of educational methods. In organizational development (see Chapter 7), one approach to investigating and changing the way people work together is for management teams to spend some days away from the workplace in which to review their practice, how they work as a team, a department or even how teams or departments work with each other.

An event of this kind might often begin with an outside consultant brought in for the purpose, summarizing what seemed to be the agenda for the time they were to spend together. He or she would probably have derived this from earlier conversations with as many participants as possible. The consultant would then make it clear that the participants were responsible for deciding how they would work through the issues: priorities; method; possible sub-groups and so on, an approach much influenced by group dynamics methods, of which more later.

The benefit of this approach is that as well as the benefit from working on live, at-work problems, the way the participants work together during the event is likely to mirror the way they work every day. The consultant can ask from time to time whether ways of working, tensions, alliances or conflicts are a unique feature of the event, or whether, as is likely, they reveal something of the way things happen at work. The participants will usually confirm or disconfirm this. The organizational simulation described in this section can be for the same purpose. As happened with the local government officers, the exercise was open enough for participants to find they had used it to express the characteristics of their day-to-day working relationships.

Influences on the interactions within a group activity from the external environment can be even more immediate, as I think the next illustration shows. It will also raise again the question for facilitators or consultants as to how to frame the interpretation or analysis of what seems to be happening in the group when the boundary between a group and its context are as blurred as this. Should the focus be on what is occurring in the here-and-now, as is often advocated in experiential group practice, or should attention be drawn to the context which it reflects? Or is this a spurious and unhelpful distinction?

## ILLUSTRATION 3:
### Experiencing social tensions through a T-group

As I mentioned briefly at the beginning of the book, sensitivity training, T (training) groups or similar forms have been used extensively since World War II. They can vary in the detail of the approach used and myths about their use abound. It is necessary to separate sense from nonsense in this area, although it must be said that some practitioners seem to do their best to make this more difficult than it should be. The design below is fairly typical of a T-group and the purpose of the group in this case is similar to the purpose of the small groups or study groups which would usually form part of a group conference as offered by the Tavistock and Grubb Institutes in the UK.

*The design.* The participants in this four-day T group were postgraduate students on a social work course. I had been invited to staff one of the groups by a course tutor I had worked with on similar events for other higher education institutions. There were three groups with about 12 students in each and each with one 'trainer' or 'consultant' experienced in this kind of work. The students were divided by us into the groups so as to ensure as heterogeneous a membership as possible in each group. The rationale for this was that differences in age, gender, work experience and other background factors influence ways of seeing and understanding; the more varied the group in these more measurable aspects, the richer the range of ideas and experience available.

*The overall purpose* of the event was described as an opportunity to learn about what happens in groups by being in one, to learn about oneself as a group member and to be able to consider the application of all this to the professional role of social worker.

The event began with an introductory session in which these aims were stated, questions responded to and the visiting staff introduced to the students. The rest of the programme for the four days consisted of three kinds of activity. Most of the sessions involved the basic small group, lasting for an hour and a half, with their purpose described as follows: 'the task of the small group is to study behaviour in the group as it happens. The role of the staff members will be to help group members in this task in any way they can'.

Implicit in this description is the assumption that the staff member is not a member of the group but works with the group in observing and making sense of what develops. The absence of any overt direction from the staff means that the participants have to work with each other in order to determine the nature and direction of the group's life over the four days. It is this involvement and the social patterns which emerge because of it, which provide the material which the group members examine in order to learn about the nature of groups.

Two other activities were interspersed with these. There were community sessions in which the whole group came together. This provided an opportunity to discuss issues of interest arising in the small groups and to experience the differences in working in this setting from the smaller groups. Also there were application groups with a membership drawn from each of the three basic small groups. The purpose of these was for the students to reflect on the observations and analysis from the small groups in relation to the wider focus of their future professional role in society. The timetable for the four days is shown in Figure 6.1.

| DAY 1 | DAY 2 | DAY 3 | DAY 4 |
|---|---|---|---|
| Introduction | T-group | Community session | T-group |
| T-group | T-group | T-group | T-group |
| T-group | Community session | Application group | Application group |
| Community session | T-group | T-group | Community session |

**Figure 6.1** *Typical timetable for a group training event*

*What happened.* For this illustration I want to describe the first small group meeting. I believe it shows again the nature of the boundary we construct between the event and the immediate context. It also demonstrates the dilemma of knowing how to make sense of an event affected by contextual factors when the aim of the group is to focus on the 'here-and-now'. Even though participants' experience of the group provides their common history — which is why so much can be learnt from it — the life of the group and what happens within it are inseparable from events outside.

The participants in the group I was working with were to have been eight women and four men. This was representative of the course population. Two of the men did not appear so that left two male participants.

At the start of the session I repeated what had been said already about the purpose of the small group and how I saw my role in working with them. As often happens, this was followed by a silence of some minutes. The topic that was eventually introduced was in stark contrast to the quiet of those early moments. The evening before, a female student living on campus had been attacked and stabbed by an intruder. She was now seriously ill in hospital. Most of that first group session was taken up with talk of the feelings of anger, of insecurity and of the revulsion that this incident had left with them. The two male students said very little during the session and one of them left at the coffee break.

## Discussion

A learning event as dramatic as this is fortunately unusual. Nevertheless, the illustration helps to explore further the nature of learning groups and of their boundaries, and of ways to account for this in working with them.

I do not remember exactly how I responded to this opening small group session but that is not important here. I remember the four days as quietly useful, covering all sorts of ground and, as often happens, left feeling it had seemed worthwhile. Certainly the event underlined the argument for there being both male and female staff to work with each group. The presence of a woman colleague, with a different experience and social history from my own and therefore a different perspective on social processes, would have strengthened the contribution from the staff team in helping the students make sense of their experience of the T group.

What are the different ways of interpreting what happened in this session and the ways a staff member could have intervened? (The various interpretations of group process considered in this section were summarized in Chapter 3.) Feelings expressed about the attack on a colleague could be interpreted as an indication that group members were anxious about the way the group might develop and about what it would be like for them over the next few days; an example of feelings arising from the here-and-now but not yet consciously associated with it. That possibility might be pointed out by the consultant in the hope of bringing the focus back into the group. It could also be put to the group that talking about the violence outside was providing a way of avoiding the initial difficulties of getting the group to work.

Equally, the consultant could draw on different ideas which would regard the content of these early exchanges as a way of exploring some of the dilemmas and dangers of making a commitment to the group; of weighing-up the possible costs of membership however desirable it might be to belong.

Somewhat different from these explanations, the preoccupation with an external event at the expense of studying what was happening in the group itself could be interpreted as the beginnings of a struggle for power and leadership within the group, particularly in challenging the consultant through thwarting the direction he apparently thought the work of the group ought to lie in. This could be pointed out too.

All these explanations appear to share in the implication that a distinction should be drawn between the group and its external world: between what goes on in the group, which is the primary focus for the event, and what has gone on or might be going on outside it, which is peripheral. In the tradition of experiential groups with their focus on the here-and-now, a preoccupation on external events is likely to be interpreted as avoidance, or an unconscious indication of people's unspoken anxieties about the group. From this perspective, thoughts in the mind of the facilitator might be:

There's some avoidance going on here. I'm beginning to feel impatient with them looking outside all the time in a way that excludes me and stops any work within the group. Ganging up on the male minority too, it wasn't their fault. They must feel very unsupported at the moment. But perhaps they're all nervous about this event. Perhaps I could point that out as a way of bringing things back into the group ... and there are some who haven't spoken at all yet.

Any of these thoughts could have been relevant during that first session but probably peripheral to the core of the group's process. To voice them might serve to reinforce the idea of the group as isolated or dislocated from its context. Similarly, to fall back on piecemeal interpretations such as whether everyone in the group is having an equal say, or to observe behaviours such as listening or interrupting, however useful at other times, would have been misplaced on this occasion. It might be more illuminating to find ways of making sense of what was happening which acknowledged the interaction between outside events and the presenting behaviour within the group.

Conversely, if the distinction between the group and its external world is made in such a way as to exclude outside events, as well as seeming to deny the validity of participants' feelings, the learning from the experience is limited. The way group members were thinking, feeling and acting in the here-and-now and the ways the group had begun to work together were as much a function of outside events as anything else brought to these early moments of the T group. There are ways in which this *connectedness* between the group and its social context can illuminate processes which recur at work, at play, within the family and in the community and provide one of the distinct advantages of using groups for learning.

From this alternative perspective, a facilitator's thoughts in the same situation might be more on these lines:

It doesn't feel good to be a heterosexual male on a morning like this. Feelings about the attack could be providing a vehicle of some kind for concerns about the group but they have certainly put power and sexuality high on the agenda at a time when we haven't yet found a way of working with such issues. What does all this bring up which will have some counterpart in the way they will work as a group and their expectations of each other – what about my role here as middle-class male? I shouldn't have agreed to be on my own. Still, there'll be experience and understanding to draw on from group members, especially the women, in sorting this out. The men must feel pretty beleaguered; no wonder the other two didn't turn up.

# The learning group as a 'small world'

In earlier chapters I have illustrated the way the boundaries drawn around group activities in designing for time, place and membership are much less clearly drawn in the participants' experience of the activity. In this section this idea is developed further. Behaviour in groups can be understood in terms of the same social and cultural patterns which pervade the wider context because they are also woven into the events of the learning group.

The T group is an effective method because the social patterns which evolve within it reflect the ways people live and work together in the rest of their everyday lives. The nature of the relationships which develop, the values and beliefs expressed in action, wanted and unwanted influences, all mirror wider social process. In this sense the T group is indeed a 'small world'.

This perspective is well described by Annie Hudson (1983). She explains the importance of understanding individual experience within a group (micro), in terms of wider social and political patterns (macro). This perspective needs emphasizing because generally speaking the field of experiential learning, because of its origins, has been more influenced by psychological than sociological ideas.

A helpful way of thinking about group methods of this kind is as a lens through which to see a clearer picture of everyday life and its murky complexities. Important aspects of social relationships are emphasized which might otherwise be taken for granted. But whether these aspects are illuminated or obscured depends on the ideas used to explain them.

The violent episode in the background to the social workers' T group undoubtedly brought into relief related attitudes which men and women show towards each other more generally. Expectations and conflicts of interest less extremely expressed would inevitably form part of the group's content, highlighted by external events but, because of this, they were more accessible to participants as learning material. Their connectedness with the social context meant that social tensions could be explored and understood in the relatively safe environment of the learning group, rather than be obscured by the spurious harmony generated in working as if such tensions have been in some magical way left outside the door.

These ideas are also relevant to less 'open' methods too. For example, a discussion group might run into difficulties because it is being dominated by a vocal minority. This could be interpreted in terms of the personality of the people involved. Concepts like 'self-effacing', 'assertive', 'deferential', or even 'demotivated', all address what is going on by focusing on individual character-istics. Alternatively, a classic group dynamics interpretation might be made in terms of the balance of forces at play, the silent majority playing as much a part as the vocal minority in maintaining the one-sided nature of the discussion.

These explanations can be applicable but on their own may obscure other explanations which take more account of the social processes involved. Is the quietness of some group members cultural in origin? (It is improper for students to speak unless invited to by the tutor.) Does it have its origins in gender differences (men being more accustomed to being granted audience and women to falling back on adopting 'men's ways' of speaking or choosing silence as the preferable alternative)? Is it based on people's beliefs about political structures (preferring hierarchy or individualistically taking advantage of more democratic settings)?

If discussion groups are to work for everyone, not just the few, this level of analysis is as useful as those which illuminate individual differences of personality. In more complex open structures such as T groups or 'learning communities', which I will describe in the next chapter, it is indispensable for tutors or participants needing to make sense of what happens within them.

# Summary

In this chapter I have used examples of more 'open' methods involving groups. The illustrations have been of activities which have less structure (rules, roles, procedures) and less tutor direction or control over scope (focus, material and theoretical frameworks used).

I have emphasized again that the boundaries of an activity as reflected in its aims and timetable do not limit participants' experience of it. In particular, I have used the illustrations to show how the *organizational context* (as in the second illustration) and the *social context* (as in the third) are mirrored in the dynamics of groups and provide a rich source of learning for individuals and work groups alike.

The implication for tutors and trainers is that the ideas we use in making sense of groups should illuminate these wider social processes. The reason for dwelling on these ideas in Chapters 4, 5 and 6, is that the broader socio-political perspective has been somewhat neglected in the development of theories for understanding groups in education and training.

## Further reading

The classic work on sensitivity training, dealing with method, underlying theories of group process and learning, research studies, issues and applications, is *T Group Theory and Laboratory Method: innovation in re-education* edited by L P Bradford, J R Gibb and K D Benne (1964). An equivalent if briefer account of the Tavistock Institute's approach to groupwork is *Learning for Leadership: interpersonal and intergroup relations* by A K Rice (1971). Both these books could equally have been suggested for further reading at the end of Chapter 3. An example of the way these methods can be applied in professional development, in this case for social work, is *Groupwork Practice* by T Douglas (1976).

As further reading on the theme of the chapter I would suggest 'The politics of experiential learning' by Annie Hudson (1983) in *Learning and Experience in Formal Education* (edited by Richard Boot and Michael Reynolds).

# 7 Groups in Education and Development

## Introduction

Having explored various issues in the theory and practice of learning groups, the aim of this chapter is to introduce applications of groupwork which are distinctive in some way. What they have in common is that they are approaches to learning and change which are at the 'cutting edge' of group practice, either because they are relatively new (as in online groups) or under constant rethinking and development. The four applications I have chosen are:

the learning community, because it is a way of basing not just a session or an event, but an entire programme on a participative approach;

online groups, groups on courses working together through the medium of computer conferencing;

single-sex groups, either in the context of T groups or for learning about gender-related issues; and

team development, as perhaps one of the best known applications of group work in organizations.

For each of these methods, there is a brief description followed by a commentary by a colleague who I know to be using or researching them.

# The learning community

'The learning community' is the name sometimes given to one of the most participative approaches to learning. Its influences are from the advocates of student-centred learning such as Carl Rogers and Malcolm Knowles. It also reflects a belief in 'community' as an ideology.

As an educational method, it has particular appeal for people involved with vocational or professional programmes where learning needs to be relevant to their work. In addition, through its emphasis on collective self-management, the learning community provides an opportunity for its members to develop social skills and an ability to take a responsible part in planning and decision making. The tutors and participants share in the control of the programme and determine together its direction and content. The notion of 'community' acknowledges that as well as the tutor's contribution, participants' skills, knowledge and experience are also available as a resource.

The essential principles of the learning community can be summarized as follows:

1) that each individual takes primary responsibility for identifying and meeting their own learning needs;
2) that each person is responsible for helping others identify and meet their needs and for offering themselves as a flexible resource to the community (Pedler, 1984).

In other words, whatever the role of tutors in initiating the programme and whatever their contribution once it has begun, its control is shared with the participants.

The reasons for using this approach are first, that people will learn more if they are able to choose to study what they see as relevant to the interests and demands arising from their professional work. Second, that students, as well as tutors, can contribute to each other's learning from their ideas and experience. Third, and reflecting wider social values, that people should have an opportunity to influence decisions which affect them, including what they learn about. The approach also accepts by implication, that what is pressing and relevant for one person's learning is not necessarily of equal interest to everyone else. Also, that if the aim is for people to manage their own learning then they need to share in the management of the procedures intended to support that learning – course structure, methods and so forth.

## How it works

With the principles of the learning community as a starting point, the tutors, in acknowledging how unusual this approach will be for many participants, might plan some activities at the beginning of the course. These activities might include:

- a discussion of the method and rationale;
- finding out about the people involved, their interests, experience and the particular skills, knowledge or expertise they can contribute to the work of the community;
- developing ideas and exploring preferences on how the members of the community will work together, not just in method but what kind of atmosphere or milieu is to be created;
- discussion of possible procedures which might be used for planning, for coordinating and for review;
- as a starting point, the staff might also give their account of what issues, ideas or topics comprise the focus for the programme.

Obviously it is not possible to describe the precise form the learning community will take because that will depend on the ideas about approach and content people bring with them and o n the way these ideas develop as the programme unfolds.

Essentially, there is an absence of tutor imposed curriculum. The curriculum in the learning community emerges from the interests of both participants and tutors. There is choice as to topic, method or approach, timing of sessions and the member-ship of groups. Some meetings may be small, 'led' by a tutor, a participant, a team, or be leader-less. Other meetings may involve the whole group, as in the review sessions which can be used to reflect on how well the programme is working for the group and for individuals.

It can be very frustrating too. The ability to plan in groups of

20 or 30 people takes time to develop, and requires a commitment to the approach which some may hold less strongly than others. Other methods of making decisions may be tried: sub-groups delegated with the responsibility; representatives; the tutor group; or if individualistic preferences outweigh collective, the community may fragment into different groups doing different things without coordinated planning of the whole.

In ways reminiscent of the organizational simulation I described in an earlier chapter, different forms emerge reflecting different values and preferences of the people taking part. It is microcosmic. There are inevitable differences to be worked with: different aims, ideas about suitable procedures, about the appropriate role for the staff, different levels of comfort with direction or the lack of it, as well as all the social, professional and cultural characteristics reflecting the day-to-day life of the larger community outside.

One thing is certain: learning communities are very demanding on tutors and participants, requiring an understanding of what happens in groups or at least a willingness to learn about it.

## Commentary

*What are the issues this approach to learning raises? In particular, what is it like to be a tutor in a learning community? We have used the learning community for some years at Lancaster University with full-time and part-time postgraduate students. I asked my colleague, Vivien Hodgson, for her thoughts on the tutor's role.*

It is easy to feel that as tutor you are not fulfilling particular expectations. It is not uncommon to feel vulnerable, exposed and deskilled. That is a bad day. On a good day you can feel exhilarated, on song and with a community that is learning – learning with a capital 'L'.

I think one of the things I learned about working with the learning community approach quite early on, and which has stayed with me, is that it is not necessarily a bad thing if people are looking unhappy, that the group is uncertain and anxious, even fearful. While I would hope these moments of anxiety and fear are temporary ones, they are arguably very useful ones, as long as they are handled with care and sensitivity. Particularly if you see learning as the process of examining who you experience yourself to be in the world and what meaning different concepts have for that view of yourself and your world, and the outcome of learning as changing the way you understand your world.

Such a view of learning is neither exclusively personal (or experiential) or exclusively cognitive (or academic). Rather it is a synthesis of both the experiential and the academic. Arguably the learning community offers an approach for encouraging such learning as it encourages participants to question their taken-for-granteds and to work with both experiential and academic knowledge.

Probably one of the most important roles that a learning community tutor has, is to keep alert to the dynamics of the community and the level of support that is being demonstrated. It is like being a support barometer. It is not necessarily being or giving the support or rescuing some individuals and chastizing others, but rather ensuring that there is an awareness of the *need for support* for all members of a learning community.

One of the problems of being a support barometer, however, is that it tends to lead to less immersion in the cut and thrust of the group's interactions. I sometimes feel distanced from the group; observing and commenting in a rather detached way. The emotional involvement feels to be of a different kind. It is the dilemma of being in there as a 'full participant' of the learning community, with supposedly no less or greater status than any other member, yet at the same time feeling duty-bound to remain sensitive to what is happening.

Arguably, all responsible members of a learning community should be both totally immersed and totally distant at one and the same time. In practice, however, this can be very hard, so I find myself veering towards the distant rather than the immersed position. This inevitably leads to a different status because, as a tutor member of a learning community, this is a legitimate stance and therefore seldom questioned. On the other hand, if a student member of a learning community takes a distant stance this is often seen as counter to the principles of a learning community and as being individualistic and/or superior.

In my view, as well as being a support barometer, a learning community tutor should also be alert to the way issues are handled and whether, as can easily be the case, participants become immersed in the experiential content of what is happening to the exclusion of the academic content.

Again, it can often be easier for the learning community tutor, through taking a more distant than immersed stance, to operate at the academic, as well as or indeed instead of, the experiential level. Particularly as it is traditionally part of a tutor's role to work with academic content. Consequently there is an ever-present danger that through fulfilling what are two key roles the learning community tutor re-asserts the authority and a power normally associated with a tutor-learner relationship in more conventional methods, which for me simply points to the real difficulties of giving up invested control and power. Do participants or tutors have the skills, awareness or desire to erode the authority of the tutor? Who will protect the learning community in the final analysis if the tutors are stripped of all authority?

These are very real issues of working with a learning community. I am only glad there is somewhere where we can work closely on such fundamental issues of power and authority in education.

## Further reading

'The dynamics of the learning community: staff intention and student experience', by Vivien Hodgson and Michael Reynolds in *Appreciating Adults Learning: from the learners' perspective*, edited by David Boud and Virginia Griffin (1987). This paper was based on in-depth interviews with students on the MA in Management Learning. As well as exploring issues which arise in using the learning community, it is an example of an evaluation which relies on students' reported experience.

# Online groups

Our part-time postgraduate programme for management teachers and trainers was designed to give them an opportunity to integrate theory from the academic world with their own professional practice. Each programme lasts for two years, during which time there are six residential events, usually of a week's duration. The thought behind this design was to provide an opportunity for fairly intensive work during each residential event, enabling participants to identify interests they would then follow up during the intervening time back at work. This activity leads to assessed papers and projects which count towards the degree. The approach is the learning community, described in the previous section.

During the period between residential events, participants meet every four or five weeks in tutorial groups, called 'sets', borrowing a term from action learning (Pedler, 1983) in recognition of the fact that whatever the tutor has to offer, as experienced professionals they contribute to each other's work out of their thinking and experience. Each set usually consists of about five students and a tutor, and a set meeting lasts a day, perhaps getting together the previous evening. Most of the day is taken up with discussing ideas for each person's assignment, although sometimes it may also be about professional or career concerns or ideas for the next residential event.

The students on this programme are very busy people. They are quite often contemplating career moves within or between organizations and live and work anywhere in the British Isles. It can be difficult to arrange times when all group members are free and, quite often, last minute work pressures mean that someone is unable to attend the tutorial group meeting.

In view of these constraints and because of our interest in developing approaches to open learning, a programme was designed in which sets would meet 'online' through the medium of computer conferencing, rather than face-to-face. In all other respects the programme's design would be the same.

## How it works

The sets form at the residential event. The size of group has been the same or sometimes slightly smaller than on the conventional programme. Using a computer from home or from work, each set member communicates with the others through telephone lines linked to the mainframe computer at the university. (I have included fuller accounts of the technology involved in the further reading section.)

As a tutor on the programme, this means that I can go online any time of day or night to respond to ideas and queries and add to discussions in progress on set members' work. The conversation is usually asynchronous which means I will be responding to comments others have made at any time since I was last 'on'. In the same way, what I say may not be replied to for a day or two. It can sometimes happen that you are online at the same time as someone else and that gets nearer to a 'normal' conversation. A set can arrange to make that happen.

But there *is* a sense of continuity to it. I am in touch with members of the group I am working with right up until the next residential event. I am also in contact with the rest of the course membership in separate 'conferences' for the whole group to exchange news from work, ideas about common concerns like assessment, or about activities for the time we next meet.

When the idea of working online was first put to me I was sceptical. I remember saying to a colleague, 'Why would anyone want to do it this way when they could meet in person?' It seemed impersonal, and I was sure I would miss the enjoyable and stimulating set meetings I had become attached to on the conventional programme. It is different, but I do not think it is of any less value. It certainly gives flexibility in time and a sense of the course as a continuing activity that a conventional part-time programme never could.

In what ways is this group a group? Are there different dynamics? Is the role of tutor different and as tutor would you need different ways of understanding the process in order to facilitate the work and ways of relating that develop? What about assessment? We practise collaborative assessment where tutor, peers and the student who did the work, all influence the final mark. What is that like when you may not know the response to your comments and judgements until some time after you make them?

## Commentary

*David McConnell has worked in the area of computer-mediated communications since 1982, at the Open University and Bath University before we persuaded him to join us at Lancaster. Here are some of his views about working with online groups.*

David began by comparing online tutorial groups on the part-time postgraduate programme with face-to-face groups on its conventional counterpart.

D: What I like about the medium is the sense of permanent contact. I'm speaking as a tutor, but I think probably everyone finds that. With face-to-face groups it's only two or three days before the meeting that you begin to think about who they (the students) are, what they are working on, what we are likely to talk about. Online, you are always in touch with who they are and what they are working on. It gives you a better sense of belonging to the group because of the element of constant contact. A face-to-face group is a group, but only for that day when it is meeting for a concentrated period, followed by a period of little or no activity as a group.

M: Is an online 'group' really a group if they don't meet face-to-face?

D: It depends what you mean by a group. There are some major differences. You can be anxious sometimes initially in a face-to-face group; it's the physical proximity. I never experience that online. When a face-to-face group re-meets, there's a period of time needed to break the ice before you feel comfortable again. Online you never experience that because there's never a dynamic of going away and coming back so there's no need to break the ice, no sense of re-meeting.

Face-to-face tutorial groups are often said to be to be closer, because, for example, they might go off to a pub for lunch together. But I feel I get to know them just as well online. People can be very forthcoming online, they talk about how they feel about assessment and I've done it myself about gay issues, talking through differences which I wouldn't feel able to in a face-to-face group.

M: What about the ideas about groups you use to make sense of what happens in them? Is that different when you are working online?

D: I think perhaps you might tend to use ideas about groups less on line than when working face-to-face.

M: Why is that?

D: Maybe because there is more time online to work out what's happening. It's more difficult to apply ideas about group behaviour because it's over a longer period of time – weeks or months. So unless you're particularly interested in tracking what's going on you may not be focusing on group process. But I am conscious of having a picture of how people work online and how they present themselves.

My assumption is that the group is always there and looking in, even if they're not saying anything, because later on people will refer to something that happened online. You weren't aware of it at the time, but clearly they were following what was happening.

M: That sounds like an illustration of the continuity you referred to earlier.

D: Yes. There are other differences too. As a tutor I sometimes feel at a loss to know how to respond, which you would never get away with in a face-to-face group. Say, at a sticky point, you'd be expected to say something in a face-to-face group. Online you might avoid it, hoping someone else might pick it up first. And often the students will.

M: What kind of sticky point?

D: Various kinds. For example, some men have a tendency online to be intellectually heavy, dense. They spend hours preparing something and it's just too much. So how do you deal with that when you know it's getting a bit oppressive?

There's another difference in that online people can look in on groups they don't belong to. It's fascinating when someone comments on a group like that. They don't have membership but they're looking in and later they may say something about it. That can't happen in face-to-face groups.

Also you can work on multiple issues. It's ok to set up new items while working on existing ones. There's no clash. There's space to say things without crashing in on other discussions. That can't happen in face-to-face groups where only one person has the floor at any one time.

M: What's the range of application of online groups?

D: Well, in the US for example, they have been used with undergraduates for economics and business studies at the New Jersey Institute of Technology (NJIT). And in organizations like Digital and IBM, conferencing is used for informal discussions and communications. At Birkbeck in the UK it's used on an occupational psychology programme. Some schools are using electronic mail to correspond internally. So it's used more for conversational aspects like seminars and tutorials than for teaching, although NJIT do use it for assignments and feedback just as you would face-to-face.

**Further reading**

David McConnell recommends two books which contain a range of papers dealing with both the technological and educational issues of using computer conferencing: A R Kaye *Collaborative Learning through Computer Conferencing* (1991), which is full of references and good papers and should be enough for anyone to get started; and L Harasim *Online Education* (1990).

# Single-sex groups

I was used to single-sex groups without calling them that when I taught organizational behaviour at a business school some 20 years ago. Nearly all of our post-experience courses were peopled exclusively by male managers and the early postgraduate groups were all male too. The design of single-sex groups as an intentional learning device was a common feature of T group work. The idea was to heighten aspects of difference between men and women and the ways this influenced what happened in the groups. The origins of this approach lay in the consciousness-raising groups of women and later, of men.

## How it works

Typically, once or twice throughout a week-long T group, there would be a session where there were all-male groups with male trainers and all-female groups with female trainers. The stated purpose for these sessions would be something like: 'The task for this session is to understand what happens when working in a group in the absence of members of the other sex'. It goes without saying that I am not clear what happened in the women's groups. The men's groups were sometimes rather dull but sometimes more intimate and more supportive than the mixed group.

What I do remember vividly is the dramatic effect single-sex group meetings had on the subsequent mixed-group sessions. Aspects of gender and sexuality were to the fore. It always seemed as if the men in the group, the way they dealt with each other and with the women, their taken-for-granteds as to their right to be influential, listened to and in positions of power, were rudely confronted. Simply put, splitting into single-sex groups was an effective way of mobilizing some consciousness amongst the women that had, up until then, been unfelt or unvoiced.

It seemed as if this was more significant than the intergroup dynamics which can develop between mixed groups: the tendency to imagine what the other group is like, to project onto it fears, envy or suspicion which have scant basis in reality, the way other groups seem more uniform, more homogeneous when seen from a distance. All of this is possible with the way single-sex groups see each other too. But there is something more: an emphasis on the significance of differences between men and women, manifested in the groups but with origins in the everyday culture and keenly felt. These sessions would often have a notable effect on the staff group too, highlighting gendered aspects of the way *they* were working together and revealing tensions of power and influence not spoken of until then.

I am aware of the current (and contentious) interest in men's groups, literature and cinema to celebrate maleness, and have included in the further reading section a paper by Richard Boot (1994). His interest is in understanding and valuing the distinctive aspects of masculinity as important in its own right, not as a backlash to feminism.

## Commentary

*For this section, I discussed single-sex groups with Ginny Hardy who works with them as an educational method and whose research agenda is concerned with women's ways of learning and knowing.*

M: What is your experience of single-sex groups?

G: If I think of the two most recent experiences of single-sex groups, the first of these was very positive. As part of a group conference there was a session called 'The Street' in which conference members had the opportunity to explore their roles within the wider community. For two hours we could do virtually anything. I opened a women's centre and gradually other women joined in until there were four or five of us. The strongest thing about it was the sense of space, the space to be ourselves, an easiness, a way of interacting without some of the stuff you get bogged down with in a mixed group.

M: What sort of stuff?

G: What comes to mind is there's no sense of having to compete to get heard, to force yourself in. It just felt easy. And we sat very near to each other, with lots of eye contact, listening, fun and laughter, we had a laugh. So there was an immediate sense of intimacy unusual in a mixed group.

M: What was the other experience?

G: That was on a women's development course. Again there was the same easiness of working together. As if there weren't issues of power. No sense of 'Who's going to control this group?' No sense of power struggle. Decisions seemed to be made easily without any sense of fuss. *And yet there was a sense of pressure to conform* to a stereotype of what women are supposed to be like – caring, supportive, emotional – and that made it difficult to be different and to speak of different aspects of femaleness which I see as just as female but which are seen as less positive by others. So I began to wonder if in mixed groups the early issues are about leadership and authority, but in women's groups they are about 'Can I be different, can I challenge others?'

M: But what do you see as the benefit of single-sex groups? What's their use? Is it only to experience this ease, the sense of space and the mutual support which goes with all that? I can see why that is useful in group conferences as a way of understanding the difference gender makes to the way people behave in groups, both for women and for men. But what about other settings? Does it have any relevance for the teacher of a geography class in school or in college?

G: Well, if you accept there *are* differences in the way women experience the world and the way they think and talk about their experience, and if you accept that in the public spheres of education and work it is men's ways which dominate, men who have the power, then single-sex groups give women the space and the opportunity to be themselves and to speak their own way and to see that as valuable in its own right – if they don't already. And that in turn influences the way women act in mixed groups to some extent.

After all, if the purpose of a group is to have a good discussion, exploratory talk – which maybe characterizes women's ways of talking more than men's – this is a good way to go about it because it encourages broadening out rather than taking fixed positions. Men's talk is more expository, showing what they know rather than exploring what *could* be known. You could argue that exploratory talk would benefit any group.

So it would be wonderful if the geography teacher could make it happen in mixed groups that both ways, women's and men's ways of knowing and talking, would operate, but working for some of the time in single-sex groups might make it more likely. It would help women value their own contribution when they were together, and then hopefully when they were in mixed groups too.

G (again): It's interesting and not insignificant that what you've chosen to focus on in talking to me is women's groups.

M: What do you mean?

G: It's as if the dominant group doesn't have to bother about this. Every group that isn't a women-only group is a 'man's group'. And yet maleness is something that men talk very little about. It's not an issue for them.

**Further reading**

'Women managers' experience of communication' by Ginny Hardy, working paper, (1993) in which she elaborates some of the ideas in the previous discussion. See also Van Nostrand (1993).

# Team development

Originally, team development was the organizational application of the T group. In the 1960s and 70s there was a trend towards a more democratic approach to organizing work and an increasing disenchantment with more hierarchical, bureaucratic methods. This change was influenced by a post-war preoccupation amongst social scientists with work group behaviour and the apparent benefits of 'democratic' leadership. I have already referred to these developments in the opening chapters. At first this shift in thinking about work was mostly in North American industrial companies but ideas and practice spread to other countries, including the UK.

Senior managers, management consultants and academics, convinced of the value of participation, encouraged teamwork, collaboration between work groups and departments and problem solving in a climate of trust, open communication and a readiness to identify and resolve conflict. Deferring to higher levels of authority was seen as a last resort. The basis of influence was to be expertise rather than seniority for its own sake.

This approach to work certainly seemed appropriate to 'Hi-tech' companies but participative management philosophy has been introduced into all kinds of organizations, public and voluntary as well as private; non-commercial as well as industrial, and into government and educational institutions.

The implications for training and development were to focus on the need for people to understand about the behaviour which went on in workgroups and teams and to develop their skills as team members. But, in contrast to learning about work behaviour on courses with people who had no day-to-day working relationship, the focus of team development is a group which actually works together.

## How it works

The groups involved in team development could be management or project teams; they might have existed for some time or be newly formed. Whole departments could be involved or there could be representatives from more than one department looking at the way they work internally and with each other. If the organization is small, everyone might be involved. The purpose for the exercise could be that the team is thought to have problems, it is facing change of some kind or to review performance to date and look for ways this could be improved.

Typically, team development takes place away from the workplace. It might last from two to five uninterrupted days and will usually involve one or more consultants, probably not members of the organization, although sometimes people with the necessary skills from a different part of the organization may be invited to work with the team.

Possible starting points for the exercise, one of which I have referred to in an earlier chapter, could be opinions gathered from individuals or groups by the consultant over the previous weeks, or an activity which the team is asked to perform with the aim of illustrating the same characteristics as the ways they usually work together; this could be a simulation or other experiential activity of the kind I have described earlier (Chapter 6). In recent years there has been an interest in work teams taking outdoor development courses together, the stresses and strains from facing physical challenges in the outdoors being used to draw parallels with behaviour at work.

There is much more variation in approaching team development than I have covered in this brief outline but the common feature is the attention given to process, to the way the group works together. It is the skill and experience in helping team members understand the significance their patterns of work highlighted during the activity which is the consultant's contribution.

## Commentary

*Richard Boot has worked in this role for different groups and for organizations and I asked him for his reflections on team development.*

RLB: There's a flavour in what you have written, of team development having only an inward-looking focus, working on the internal functioning of the team and how its members relate to one another. In the 1970s, when I became involved in this kind of work, it's true that there did seem to be a preoccupation with internal operations, as if a team existed in some kind of vacuum, almost independent of the task. I know there *are* still people who do team development who only look at interpersonal relationships, but that's inadequate without also looking at task effectiveness.

There's more of a need to look at how the team as a whole functions in relation to its environment. Not *instead of* looking internally, but *as well as*.

M: What are you thinking of as a team's environment?

RLB: It could be anything from other parts of the organization the team relates to, or the market place the organization is part of, or the community, or indeed any organization or individual that has a stake in their operation, makes demands on them, or imposes constraints on what they do.

M: If you are working with a team, then, how would you go about it?

RLB: My view is that for effectiveness, team development needs to address three categories of questions and the interrelationship between them (RLB is referring to a framework he has developed for working with teams, see Figure 7.1). The aim is to get a balance between looking out and looking in.

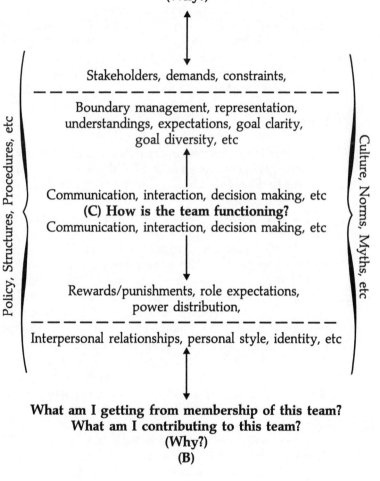

**Figure 7.1** *A framework for team development*

*M:*     Specifically?

*RLB:*   Well, next week for instance I'm working with the board of an organization for a day – incidentally the two to five days you refer to seems somewhat luxurious – people are unlikely to give up that amount of time these days. After talking with the chief executive I have sent questions based on the framework to each team member. They will consider these questions and should come prepared and primed for the meeting. Ideally I would talk to each of them first. I've asked them to think about how they relate to the questions and their answers will provide the material we shall work with.

*M:*     So what are you hoping for out of this?

*RLB:*   To look at the differences in their views, working towards establishing a common view of what the team is for, what it exists to do and deciding on the criteria for deciding if it has been successful.

*M:*     And is this the kind of team development you are doing at the moment?

*RLB:*   Mostly it's a continuous relationship. I would spend one or two days like this with a team every six months or so and then, occasionally, we might devote a session to explore in more depth a particular issue which has emerged. So, for example, one company I'm working with has just signed up for Opportunity 2000 (a government initiative to encourage equal opportunities for women at all levels in organizations). This team has made this a priority for themselves and decided to look at how gender issues work their way out in their own functioning. So, at a special session, each brought a subordinate of the opposite sex and looked at how Opportunity 2000 affected how they worked with the rest of the organization and with the issues it surfaced about how they worked with each other – as men and women.

*M:*     I have set this team development in the context of learning groups. Would you see it that way?

*RLB:*   Yes. At two levels. They're learning about the functioning and patterns of the team and, more significantly, learning the habit of being aware of these questions while they're operating and of addressing issues which arise as a result.

And there's another level. It's developing a common language so they can talk to each other about how they work together, about their goals and criteria for success.

M:      Is your knowledge of group behaviour useful in all this?

RLB:    Yes. In fact I'd say it was an essential prerequisite to this kind of work; but it's also more systemic. I would draw on wider organizational theory as well to take account of the context the team is working in.

# 8  Postscript

Illustrations in the previous chapters have introduced different applications of group methods from the considerable range available to teachers or trainers wishing to add to more traditional approaches to learning. I have used these examples to demonstrate some of the ideas useful in designing group activities and in making sense of what can result from using them. Some of the points I have emphasized are these:

- Group activities involve participants and tutors in more complex processes than other teaching methods. Whatever the intended purpose of a group activity, people's experience of it is more varied than could be predicted from the design. Specifically:
  - the experience of being a member of a learning group consists of thoughts and feelings about the working relationships which evolve, as well as about the academic focus for the activity.
  - as with any experiential method, whatever its specific aim or purpose, participants will also make connections with other past or current events and associated concerns and hopes, joys and disappointments.
  - just as ideas learned through any teaching method last beyond the course or event which introduced them, so too will the processes generated during a group activity (feelings about the group, loyalties, antipathies, feelings of achievement and so on).

  (These aspects of group methods are discussed in Chapter 4.)
- When working with group methods it is worth remembering that:
  - although much of the participants' experience of a group

activity is hidden, some of this experience may be personally or educationally significant none the less (Chapter 4).

- participants can be learning from any of these personal and social processes and even from the values embodied in the method itself. This learning may or may not be intended by the person using a group activity and may or may not be consistent with their aim in using it (Chapters 5 and 6).
- the dynamics of a group inevitably reflect broader social and cultural processes as well as the educational or organizational context (Chapter 6).

- In selecting ideas and theories about groups and group work, it is important to bear in mind that theory, like education generally, is never value-free. Ideas about groups applied to this field show a preponderance of psychological perspectives at the expense of sociological ones – an imbalance which favours an individualistic view of the world.

Two further aspects of using group methods are worth thinking about, and I mention them here briefly in conclusion. They concern opportunity for development and questions raised by assessment for working with groups.

# Implications for staff development

A point I made at the outset was that people intending to use group methods need to develop the skills and understanding essential for designing and running them. This can be only partly achieved through acquiring a theoretical foundation. Understanding the experience of groupwork and group membership and the ambiguities of the tutor's role in participative approaches is best acquired through working with professional colleagues, through reflecting on one's own practice of groupwork and through taking part in experiential methods of the kind I have illustrated (T groups, learning communities or group conferences – see the 'Further reading' section in Chapter 3 for addresses of provider associations). These methods, in the hands of people who know what they are doing, are probably the most effective source of tutor development in acquiring the skills and understanding necessary for group work.

# Implications of assessment

An aspect of using learning groups I have not touched on in previous chapters is assessment. Group methods involve students and trainees in a richer, if less predictable, experience. The content of this experience is personal and social as well as intellectual. In recognition of this I have argued for control of learning to be shared between staff and participants. But if, as is usual, the tutor or trainer has ultimate responsibility for assessment, how do they take account of this in shaping the processes of choice and control in the classroom?

It may not seem realistic or appropriate to introduce more collaborative forms of assessment or appraisal – although to do so would be more consistent in programmes based on participative methods – but an awareness of this aspect should at least inhibit tutors or trainers from passing themselves off as 'group members'. (An excellent discussion of the implications of assessment for working with structured exercises can be found in the Jeff Hearn article cited in the 'Further reading' section of Chapter 4.)

Finally, I would restate my intention in writing this account of group methods in education and training, which is to encourage interest and understanding in learning groups while emphasizing their complexity in practice.

# Bibliography

Asch, S (1952) 'Effects of group pressure upon the modification and distortion of judgements', in Swanson, G E, Newcomb, T M and Hartley, E L (eds), *Readings in Social Psychology* (2nd edn.) New York: Holt, Rinehart and Winston.

Bales, R F (1950) *Interaction Process Analysis: a method for the study of small groups*, Chicago: University of Chicago Press.

Bavelas, A (1951) 'Communication patterns in task-oriented groups', in Laswell, H and Lerner, D, *The Policy Sciences*, Stanford, Calif: Stanford University Press.

Bernstein, B (1971) 'On the classification and framing of educational knowledge', in Young, M F D (ed) *Knowledge and Control*, London: Collier-MacMillan.

Binsted, D (1980, 1981) 'The design of learning events for management, parts 1 and 2', *Management Education and Development*, August, 1980, Spring, 1981.

Bion, W (1961) *Experiences in Groups*, London: Tavistock.

Boot, R L (1994) 'Management learning and the white male heritage', in Tanton, M (ed), *Women in Management*, London: Routledge (in press).

Boot, R L and Reynolds, M (eds) (1983a) *Learning and Experience in Formal Education*, Manchester Monographs, Manchester University.

Boot, R L and Reynolds, M (1983b) 'Issues of control in simulations and games', *Simulation/Games for Learning*, **13**, 1, Spring, 3–9.

Boot, R L and Reynolds, M (1984) 'Rethinking experience based events' in Cox, C and Beck, J (eds) *Management Development: Advances in Practice and Theory*, London: Wiley.

Bradford, L P, Gibb, J R and Benne, K D (eds) (1964) *T Group Theory and Laboratory Method: Innovation in Re-education* New York: Wiley.

Cooper, C (ed.) (1975) *Theories of Group Processes*, Chichester: Wiley.

Dewey, J (1910) *How We Think*, New York: DC Heath.

Dewey, J (1916 and 1966) *Democracy and Education*, New York: Free Press.

Douglas, T (1976) *Groupwork Practice*, London: Tavistock/ Routledge.

Dyer,W G (1997) *Team Building: issues and alternatives*. Reading, Mass: Addison-Wesley.

Freire, P (1972) *Pedagogy of the Oppressed*, Harmondsworth: Penguin.

Harasim, L (ed.) (1990) *Online Education*, New York: Praeger.

Hardy, G (1993) 'Women managers' experience of communication', working paper, Department of Management Learning, Lancaster University.

Hastings, C, Bixby, P and Chaudhry-Lawton, R (1986) *Superteams*, Glasgow: Collins.

Hearn, J (1983) 'Issues of control in simulations and games: a reconsideration', *Simulation/Games for Learning*, **13**, 3, Autumn, 120–25.

Hill, W F (1977) *Learning Thru Discussion*, London: Sage.

Hodgson, V E (1984) 'Learning from lectures', in Marton, F, Hounsell, D and Entwistle, N (eds) *The Experience of Learning*, Edinburgh: Scottish Academic Press.

Hodgson, V E and Reynolds, M, (1980) 'Participants' experience as the basis of course improvement', *Management Education and Development*, **11**, 210–18.

Hodgson, V E and Reynolds, M (1981) 'The hidden experience of learning events: illusions of involvement', *Personnel Review*, **10**, 1, 26–9.

Hodgson, V E and Reynolds, M (1987) 'The dynamics of the learning community: staff intention and student experience' in Boud, D and Griffin, V (eds), *Appreciating Adults Learning: from the learner's perspective*, London: Kogan Page.

Hudson, A (1983) 'The politics of experiential learning', in Boot, R L and Reynolds, M (eds) *Learning and Experience in Formal Education*, Manchester Monographs, Manchester University.

Jaques, D (1991) *Learning in Groups*, London: Kogan Page.

Joyce, B and Weil, M (1972) *Models of Teaching*, Hemel

Hempstead: Allyn and Bacon.

Kaye, A R (ed.) (1991) *Collaborative Learning through Computer Conferencing*, Berlin: Springer-Verlag.

Knowles, M (1975) *Self-directed Learning: a guide for learners and teachers*, Chicago: Association Press.

Kolb, D A (1984) *Experiential Learning*, Englewood Cliffs, NJ: Prentice-Hall.

Kolb, D A and Fry, R E (1975) 'Toward an applied theory of experiential learning' in Cooper, C (ed.) *Theories of Group Processes*, London: Wiley.

Kolb, D A, Rubin, I M and McIntyre, J M (1984) *Organizational Psychology, an experiential approach to organizational behavior*, Englewood Cliffs, NJ: Prentice-Hall.

Lippit, R and White, R K, 'An experimental study of leadership and group life', in Maccoby, E E, Newcomb, T M and Harley, E L (eds), *Readings in Social Psychology* (3rd edn.), New York: Holt.

McCollom, M (1990) 'Re-evaluating group development: a critique of the familiar models', in Gillette, J and McCollom, M (eds). *Groups in Context*, Reading, Mass: Addison-Wesley.

Palmer, B W M (1979) 'The study of the small group in an organizational setting', in Babington Smith, B and Farrell, B A (eds) *Training in Small Groups*, Oxford: Pergamon.

Parlett, M and Hamilton, D (1977) 'Evaluation as illumination: a new approach to the study of innovatory programmes', in Hamilton, D, Jenkins, D, King, C, MacDonald, B and Parlett, M (eds) *Beyond the Numbers Game*, London: Macmillan.

Pedler, M (1983) *Action Learning in Practice*, Aldershot: Gower.

Pedler, M and Boydell, T (1984) *Developing the Learning Community*, Aldershot: Gower.

Pedler, M (1994) 'Developing the learning community', in Pedler, M and Boydell, T (eds) *Management Self-development: concepts and practices*, London: Gower.

Potter, S (1978) 'A social history of the 'T' group', *Group Relations*, November.

Reynolds, M (1982) 'Learning the ropes', *Society*, **19**, 6, Sept/Oct 30–34.

Rice, A K (1971) *Learning for Leadership: interpersonal and intergroup relations*, London: Tavistock.

Rioch, M J (1975) 'The work of Wilfred Bion on groups' in Colman, A D and Bexton, W H (eds) *Group Relations Reader 1*, Washington: A K Rice Institute.

Roethlisberger, F J and Dickson, W J (1939) *Management and the Worker*, Cambridge, Mass: Harvard University Press.

Rogers, C (1969) *Freedom to Learn*, Columbus, OH: Charles E Merrill.

Schein, E H (1969) *Process Consultation: its role in organization development*, Reading, Mass: Addison-Wesley.

Smith, P B (ed) (1980) *Small Groups and Personal Change*, London: Methuen.

Trist, E L and Bamforth, K W (1951) 'Some social and psychological consequences of the long-wall method of coal-getting', *Human Relations*, **4**, 3–38.

Tuckman, B W (1965) 'Developmental sequences in small groups', *Psychological Bulletin*, **54**, 229–49.

Van Nostrand, C H (1993) *Gender-responsible Leadership: detecting bias, implementing interventions*, London: Sage.

# Index